*STANDING ON
SHOULDERS:*

A LEADER'S GUIDE TO
DIGITAL
TRANSFORMATION

STANDING ON SHOULDERS:

A LEADER'S GUIDE TO

DIGITAL

TRANSFORMATION

JACK MAHER AND
CARMEN DeARDO

It is our turn to take what we've been given and take it to the next level

ARCHWAY PUBLISHING

For commercial use permission/release, to report broken or updated links, and for additional or updated information, please visit and contact us at https://StandingOnShoulders.us

Archway Publishing books may be ordered through booksellers or by contacting:

Archway Publishing
1663 Liberty Drive
Bloomington, IN 47403
www.archwaypublishing.com
1 (888) 242-5904

Interior Image Credit: Jack Maher and Carmen DeArdo

ISBN: 978-1-4808-6979-0 (sc)
ISBN: 978-1-4808-6980-6 (e)

Library of Congress Control Number: 2018912215

Print information available on the last page.

Archway Publishing rev. date: 1/23/2019

CONTENTS

FOREWORD

I've had the privilege and pleasure of studying Carmen DeArdo's work and ideas for five years. When I first met him, I was immediately impressed by two things: his humility and his singular focus on modernizing the architectural and technical practices at Nationwide Insurance.

I think it's a testament to his vision and perseverance that the values and practices that he's been advocating for years have increasingly been adopted in an organization that relies on the work of over 8,000 technologists.

Of course, this is not easy — it requires successfully influencing those who do the work, who may be skeptical, too busy, or aren't allowed to by their leadership. Changing the way people work at any scale requires understanding the goals and aspirations of all these groups, understanding the obstacles they face, helping them see how those obstacles can be overcome, and of course, giving them all the credit for the benefits they create.

On behalf of everyone who tries to improve the business outcomes of the technology work we do every day, I applaud the efforts taken and the writing of this book, so others can replicate their amazing outcomes. This book fulfills the promise of documenting their journeys and lessons learned, and showing how the promise of creating world-class technology organizations can be within the reach of everyone.

Gene Kim
Portland, OR
June 2018

INTRODUCTION

In 1159 John of Salisbury wrote in his Metalogicon, "Bernard of Chartres used to compare us to dwarfs perched on the shoulders of giants. He pointed out that we see more and farther than our predecessors, not because we have keener vision or greater height, but because we are lifted up and borne aloft on their gigantic stature." [1]

Standing on Shoulders looks at how we can apply the lessons that have been hard won in the past to our current challenges and needs. We're at a crossroads where we are seeing and doing things that were inconceivable just a few years ago. Change is increasing in both frequency and amplitude, and if we're not changing, we will not survive. The good news, however, is that we have everything we need not only to survive but to thrive, and the lessons are time-tested and well-proven. That seems incongruous with the fact that technology has created this situation, but this is a classic case of old school meets new school, and the synergy is nothing short of amazing.

Transforming our organizations to be competitive (and thrive) in today's digital age requires a unique combination of "old world thinking" of quality, differentiation (based on creativity), and uniqueness (based on better serving your market than the competition), and "new world thinking" of meeting your market where they want you to be. Making your organization "digital" is a lot more than just creating a compelling mobile app and "moving to the cloud." To thrive in the new marketplace, you need to think and act differently, in a meaningful and ultimately liberating way. The digital age "lowers the water level," exposing the rocks

---

[1] <*https://en.wikipedia.org/wiki/Standing_on_the_shoulders_of_giants*>

that were under the surface before, making your shortcomings not just visible but unavoidable. You must remove (or at least smooth) those rocks and reduce the bumps and turbulence that impede the flow of value from the source to the recipient.

The concepts here start before the Industrial Revolution, in some cases even further back. We build on the time-proven approach of writing down what you do, measuring it, and validating the process and results. These practices have deep roots including time-motion studies of Frederick Taylor and Frank and Lillian Gilbreth, WW2 logistics systems, and more recently the Toyota Production System, and Agile software development. Each lends a piece of their core to our newest chapter—the Digital Revolution.

Be the willow, not the oak.

Better still, learn from the masters. Don't learn the hard way.

Get more information, updated and expanded content, and access resources to help you plan and execute your transformation at https://StandingOnShoulders.us.

How to Use This Book

This book will help mid- to senior-level leaders to evaluate and implement changes that will enable or drive their organization's digital transformation. It offers insight into

- *Why* cultural norms, behaviors, and expectations need to be considered (and likely modified) across our organization(s)
- *What* needs to change and the basics of planning a successful transition from current state to future state in a sustainable way
- *How* to execute the change(s), whether it's a hard pivot for survival or an evolutionary program in phases over time to ensure you remain competitive

Standing on Shoulders pulls from firsthand experience of two thought leaders who developed and led the digital transformation of IT practices within a Fortune 100 company. This was the culmination of years of successful delivery and preparation for the challenge. The supporting ideas, authors, and other resources used are provided directly and via direct references for further exploration as desired. Everything you need to know and understand to determine what you need/want to do and to actually do it is all right here for direct application.

You and your leadership may already know that you need to do some or even all these things. Articulating what needs to be done and answering the probing questions of why, and being able to satisfy boards, investors, and other senior leaders, can be vexing and requires thoughtful responses. Just as the purchasing agent asks all the questions to the salesperson to prepare that individual to represent the opportunity within their organization, you need to be conversant on the who, what, why, when, and how of the transformation if you hope to get the resources you will need.

The How section provides information regarding tools and services that will help you target the right vendors quickly should you need to make a change to your technology landscape. The options will also consider small-, medium-, and large-sized efforts/organizations/approaches to right-size your approach for your organization's size, complexity, and appetite for both technology and transformation.

I. WHY

Digital transformation is arguably the flavor of the day and likely will be for a long time. Finally, here is a "fad" you can get behind and make your own. Doing so will either propel your organization to the top of your industry or enable your ongoing existence. Is this merely hype and exaggeration? In a word, no. Unless you are alone in your marketplace, your competition will do this, and failing to act will mean the end of your organization as you know it. Today's marketplace is not satisfied with the status quo; they want performance and delivery that we previously considered unfeasible.

Feature-rich capabilities that expand daily, user-centric ecosystems where needs are anticipated and provided, customizable experiences that respond to our input and circumstances, and immediate and continuous availability are now expectations thanks to the "unicorns": Amazon, Etsy, Pinterest, and Google, as well as savvy brick-and-mortar companies that have become digital "horses" (like Disney, Nordstrom, and Capital One). IBM has shown that "elephants can dance,"[2] and you must also.

"What's in it for me?" you might be asking. Survival. But there's a lot more too, including truly engaged and satisfied associates and customers alike. Right now, it is possible to achieve performance that will thrill your board and clients and drive new opportunities and growth beyond what you think. Hang on tight, because this will be a bumpy ride, but it will be a fun one, and you can make the difference you've dreamed of a reality.

---

[2] https://www.ibm.com/developerworks/rational/library/2071.html

What Is Lean, Do I Need Agile, and What is DevOps and Why Should I Use It?

Would you like that cheaper, faster, *and* better? Yes, please!

It used to be said that you could pick any two from faster, better, and cheaper. But that's not an option anymore. Today, if you want to survive let alone thrive, you need all three. Lean, Agile, and DevOps: when put together, they drive a synergy that delivers benefits that were unattainable before today.

This book is intended to provide organizations a guide to understanding the value of these popular "movements" of today and a roadmap for an effective transformation from where you are to what you want to be. You may only want to do part of this, or perhaps do parts over time, before committing completely.

"Faster" and "cheaper" are relatively straightforward and easy to measure. But what do we mean by "better"? Better will have both "hard" and "soft" components, and it can be measured as well. Examples of these components are fewer defects, higher customer satisfaction, improved engagement of associates, stronger compliance with standards, and better alignment of activities and outcomes with organizational goals and desired outcomes.

Most lean initiatives are typically focused on making a process more efficient and removing waste (*muda*). Reduced cost is a direct result of lean practices from multiple perspectives. But wait; there's more! Most of the lean practices will also lead to increased flow and speed of delivery, but that is often considered a secondary result. As a result, the emphasis on reducing financial costs sometimes becomes a local optimization and doesn't necessarily improve flow through the value stream and increase the speed of delivery. We're going to look at all this (Lean, Agile, and DevOps) in a concerted approach that leverages the strengths of each and creates a synergy that is more powerful than just the sum of the pieces.

Lean —Eliminating Waste, Consistency, Visual, Flow

Lean is almost always traced back to the Toyota Production System, but, of course, the roots go much deeper. We can trace a direct line from Henry

Ford's assembly line and even earlier. But in the 1990s, another "turn of the crank" helped define the principles that have helped many organizations in many kinds of business apply the concepts to what they do:

- Specify the value desired by the customer
- Identify the value stream for each product, providing that value and challenging all the wasted steps currently necessary to provide it
- Make the product flow continuously through the remaining value-added steps
- Introduce pull between all steps where continuous flow is possible
- Manage toward perfection so that the number of steps and the amount of time and information needed to serve the customer continuously falls[3]

Waste

Eliminating as much waste as possible is the lowest-hanging fruit of all. This is an area where there is essentially no downside and little resistance will be met.

A great place to get started is to begin to identify and eliminate waste so your precious resources are focused on positive returns. The widely used acronym DOWNTIME can help us identify and remember the eight kinds of waste that are our primary targets.[4]

D   defects
O   overproduction
W   waiting
N   non-utilized
T   transportation
I   inventory
M   motion
E   extra processing

---

[3] https://www.lean.org/WhatsLean/History.cfm
[4] https://goleansixsigma.com/8-wastes/

Defects	Efforts caused by re-work, scrap, and incorrect information
Overproduction	Production that is more than needed or before it is needed
Waiting	Wasted time waiting for the next step in a process
Non-utilized talent	Underutilizing people's talents, skills, knowledge, innovation or capabilities
Transportation	Unnecessary movements of products and materials
Inventory	Excess products or materials not being processed
Motion	Unnecessary movements by people (e.g., walking or carrying)
Extra processing	More work or higher quality than is required by the customer

Consistency

> Consistency is the mark of a champion
>
> —Unknown

When we act and perform consistently, we become predictable. This predictability is the baseline for our performance.

At a recent conference at the Center of Operational Excellence at Ohio State University,[5] we had the opportunity to participate in a team-building event. This fun event focused on the benefits of taking a focused approach to getting work done. "The PIT Experience"[6] focuses on the fundamentals of lean, such as minimizing wasted motion, defects, *takt* time versus speed, and other key concepts. Part of the mantra is to "go slow to go fast," which seems counterintuitive. But as we each gained consistency in performing our part and learned to count on the others to do their part, we got better and faster. We must take the time and invest in the effort to develop our skills to be proficient, with our hands

---

[5] https://fisher.osu.edu/centers-partnerships/coe
[6] http://theleantoolbox.com/services/lean-education/the-pit-experience/

and otherwise. We frequently refer to this as building "muscle memory." Here's a quick video that shows the evolution of pit crews in Formula 1 racing:

> https://youtu.be/aLHDc3ik2ZE
> "Formula 1 pit stops evolution - 50s, 70s, 80s, 90s, 00s, 10s (slowest to fastest)."

It is amazing to see how the speed has improved along with the crispness of execution as crews have made continuous process improvements over the years.

In his book *Outliers: The Story of Success,*[7] Malcolm Gladwell investigates what it takes to become an expert. He examines world-class performers and walks us through to the realization that it takes in the order of ten thousand hours to become an expert at a complex subject. We learn from an early age that if we want to become good at something, we must learn the basics and then "practice, practice, practice." In a *Forbes* article on leadership, Ian Altman connects the dots from being a world-class performer or athlete to applying these skills to business.[8] Whether it is sales training, quality inspection, or driving, we know that experience—doing the same thing over time and in varying conditions—teaches us how, when, and where to focus our attention, how to anticipate where problems tend to occur, and how to adapt for minor or controllable variations.

In fact, we can combine all three of these sources and distill a directly applicable approach to how we design our work and focus our resources. Later, we'll talk about designing processes for resiliency and speed and how we can take a deterministic approach to our design that will enable automation. For now, let's focus on the fact that we can decompose the processes that we execute, from complicated to simple, by breaking them down into smaller pieces, just as the pit crews do.

There are other benefits to the individual and the team. As we

---

[7] https://www.amazon.com/Outliers-Story-Success-Malcolm-Gladwell/dp/0316017930
[8] https://www.forbes.com/sites/ianaltman/2015/03/31/how-to-build-muscle-memory-for-business-success/#589b79e414a7

become more proficient and more predictable in delivering our piece of the solution, we become more confident. Our confidence not only makes us feel better, but it helps us to deliver better.[9] From a "self" perspective, confidence based on competence helps us focus on the right things; it helps us maintain our motivation to deliver well and strive for even better performance. The positivity within becomes self-reinforcing and soon becomes contagious as others see that they can count on us. This confidence helps us avoid self-defeating behaviors and defensiveness when others ask for more of us, and it helps us improve the overall process. Confidence fuels our resiliency when events take an unexpected turn or when external factors require a change.

When our teammates become more comfortable and begin to realize that they can count on our consistency to deliver, they can spend less time being worried about what they'll "get" and center their attention on their part. When they don't have to worry about what they'll get from us, they can be fully invested in delivering their "A game." The confidence contagion builds team *esprit de corps* and elevates teams, fostering an environment of performance and making success more likely. This creates a self-reinforcing cycle of validation of positivity.

> *The greatest waste in America is failure to use the abilities of people.*
> —W. Edwards Deming

> Carmen: In 2014, I was introduced to an amazing community of DevOps leaders through my association with Gene Kim's organization IT Revolution[10]. This started with an invite from Hayden Lindsey to speak with him at Gene's inaugural DevOps Enterprise Summit. At the time, I didn't realize this would introduce me to amazing group of leaders like Jason Cox (Disney), Courtney Kessler (Nike), Sam Guckenheimer (Microsoft), Paula Thrasher (CSRA), Mik Kersten (Tasktop), John

---

[9] https://www.psychologytoday.com/blog/the-power-prime/201011/business-confidence-matters-in-the-corporate-world

[10] https://itrevolution.com/

Willis and Nicole Forsgren (noted authors of books like *The DevOps Handbook*), Topo Pol (Capital One), Ross Clanton (Verizon), Dominica DeGrandis, Mark Schwartz (AWS), John Allspaw, Scott Prugh (CSG), Rosalind Radcliffe (IBM), Terri Potts, and many others. What struck me was not the fact that these folks were brilliant in all realms of technology but that a core motivation for their passion was to improve the lives of the millions of folks for which IT was their profession. I quickly realized that Gene and this broader community wanted to provide a service to create and sustain the capability for those in this profession, not only to thrive professionally and grow but also to have a life where they had time for their other passions, like family, friends, and community involvement. I learned that true leadership means not only focusing on your customers but also striving to provide this type of experience for those you lead.

Visibility—Putting Light and Focus on the Work

Making work visible is a theme that we'll explore more thoroughly later in this book. But for now we'll focus on some of the fundamental components and will look at "planned" work. Because this part is so important and informs everything else we do, we're going to skip ahead to a little bit of the How here and begin creating our value-stream map.

In *The Mothman Prophesies*,[11] the "expert" character in the movie, Alexander Leek (played by Alan Bates), makes the following observation: "If there was a car crash ten blocks away, that window washer up there could probably see it. Now, that doesn't mean he's God, or even smarter than we are. But from where he's sitting, he can see a little further down the road."

The first step of making work visible is to understand what work is being done, who is doing that work, and where we can find it. There's no

---

[11] https://www.imdb.com/title/tt0265349/characters/nm0000869?ref_=ttfc_fc_cl_t24

"rocket science" here, but there may be more detective work than you might think.

Step 1: Identify Your Value Stream

Value-stream mapping is a lean-management method for analyzing the current state and designing a future state for the series of events that take a product or service from its beginning through to the customer.[12] Value-stream mapping is deceptively easy. Like so many other skills, even games, such as Othello, whose motto is "a minute to learn, a lifetime to master,"[13] it is quite simple conceptually. Implementation can be challenging to say the least. It is not the intent of this book to instruct or guide the development of value-stream mapping, which is the documentation and analysis of a value chain.[14] However, Appendix A will help you understand what is involved. As with our journey to technical competence, the fundamentals are straightforward. There are many resources on the web and in real life that will help you begin this process. The most important thing is to start the process, even if it is simplistic at first. You can get better and more elaborate as you go. In fact, "progressive elaboration" should begin here if it's not in your "toolbox" already. Your value-stream map should begin at your "intake" of work, when the work is requested or identified.

Understanding and being able to articulate and analyze the value delivered and the steps or processes involved in creating and delivering value are essential to being successful in an increasingly competitive marketplace. We cannot overstate the importance of doing this well and having teams that understand the concept of the value stream.

Most importantly, teams must be taught concepts that help them continuously identify roadblocks to delivering more quickly. Key to this is the lean concept of value-stream analysis. If you walk up to a team and ask them why they can't go faster, they will typically say they are waiting for something. They could be waiting for more work to flow into their

---

[12] https://en.wikipedia.org/wiki/Value_stream_mapping
[13] Othello and A Minute to Learn...A Lifetime to Master are Registered Trademarks of Anjar Co., ©1973, 2004 Anjar Co. and title of a book on the topic by Brian Rose
[14] https://en.wikipedia.org/wiki/Value_chain

backlog. They could be waiting for infrastructure necessary for development or testing. Or they could be waiting for another team to develop a service they need to consume.

Many teams don't spend time in retrospectives talking about how to overcome these types of blockers or wait states and developing counter-measures as continuous-improvement initiatives. One reason for this is the lack of objective data that can be analyzed to provide insights on this. This is where the lead-time metric comes into play. Once teams are provided with this measure, broken into process times for development and testing and wait times, as noted above, they can then determine what counter-measures or continuous-improvement initiatives will accelerate their ability to deliver.

While you are building your value-stream map, pay attention to those areas where you think you are particularly good and those where you are not so good. Ask yourself (and your leaders and associates),

- What do we really care about?
- What is it that gives us a competitive advantage in the marketplace?
- How do the things we really *care about* and the things we are *good at*, giving give us a competitive advantage, align?

How do our capabilities and shortfalls square with our culture?

An accurate self-assessment is crucial, because this will be our foundation for all the remaining steps. It will set the stage and be integral to delivering both better and faster (and those two will drive "cheaper").

Step 2: Put Your Value-Stream Map up on a Wall

Putting your value-stream map on the wall is the first step in making the work visible. It can be scary putting this out there for inspection by anyone who might walk by. Consider this as you select where to post your map. It might contain information that you deem proprietary and confidential. Therefore, the selection of where to post this should consider physical security, operational security, and information security. On the other hand, there is a significant risk-reward relationship here. Posting it in your lobby may not be the best choice. Instead, you might select the company cafeteria, where all associates can see it and share feedback. Or perhaps you might place it in the executive conference room, where only mid-level managers and senior leaders have access. Your organizational culture, the type of work or market in which you operate (e.g., national defense, consumer goods, regulated services) and the value you place on collaboration will largely determine the appropriate placement and level of sharing.

Initially, this will be an "academic" approach, meaning that you will identify the steps and processes at a high level without identifying the actual work that is currently in process at each step or section of your value-stream map.

Do you have any SLAs (service-level agreements) or other metrics or measurements that guide or specify entrance or exit criteria, expected time to process or deliver? You should identify the "control points" along the way, including any inspections, validations, or reporting opportunities that reflect the state, quality, or condition of the product or intermediate work product(s).

Once you have completed your first draft, how will you validate that you've captured it all? There are several ways, and you should exercise at least a couple of different approaches to ensure you've covered the basics. The first is as simple as a "sniff test." In a review of the process from beginning to end with more than one "internal expert," does the flow make sense? Does the process cover at least all the "big chunks" of the process and flow from end to end? Are sections or components overly simplified for ease of documentation so that the significant steps are obscured? There's certainly no need or desire to specify down to the step-by-step execution level, but a good target is the team level, component level, or subassembly level.

Another suggested step would be to have the next-level-down managers and supervisors review your map. They will be able to look more closely at the transitions and handoffs between business and operational units. They can also begin to point out areas that are currently challenged and where problems are generally introduced or identified.

In God we trust. All others bring data.
—W. Edwards Deming

When the work is visible, we can see what is going on, and we ask questions like "Why is this stuck here?" and "Why are you even working on that?" Visible work also drives ownership and accountability. Often, we simply have too much work going on at once. We're trying to multi-thread and multi-task, but, just like with our highways and networks, the more "traffic," the slower everything goes.

Visual management systems (VMS) are a key component of most lean implementations. The reason why is very straightforward. We put the most important measurements of what we're doing up on the wall, where everyone can see them. What's our priority? It's right up there on the wall!

Visual management eliminates much unnecessary work and significantly enhances communications. Status reports become a relic of the past because our status is always visible. With small teams and single-location organizations, this can be quite simple and very low tech. A whiteboard in every team space is the minimum table stake here. In fact, we should plan and prepare for multiple whiteboards in each team space to enable the multitude of needs:

- Status and work management
- Collaboration and concept development
- Dependencies, open items, and parking lot

Flow—it is the hardest part to get and arguably the most important. When we go into a manufacturing or production facility these days, the flow of materials and products through the facility should be immediately evident. Most facilities today are specifically designed to enhance flow.

There are multiple models for how work flows, but generally we can identify them as either "push" or "pull." A push model is characterized by an input or prior piece of work being presented to the next team or step, which is then expected to begin executing their step or part of the process immediately. A pull model, on the other hand, is characterized by a team retrieving from a backlog or other queue the next piece of work to be addressed, based on priority and capacity. Kanban is based on the pull model.

Many studies have been undertaken to look at how work flows best. Pushing work to a team has several downsides, generally due to a high likelihood of mismatched rates of feed versus consumption. Just like the classic *I Love Lucy* episode in the candy factory,[15] we are quite likely to "overfeed" and create too much WIP, or work in progress. We know that the more work an individual or team has, the slower the progress is. While today's processors may be able to handle time-slicing well, we humans do not. When we switch from one task to another, we must execute a context switch: we must clear our mind of the prior task and reorient our thinking with the new task.

Similarly, if we rely on a push state, we will occasionally leave the team without sufficient work. In other words, we starve them. Neither is good.

Instead, we should have a "pile" of stuff to do, along with the right information and resources to be able to pull the highest-priority work from the pile and begin to complete the work. For a team or line, we call this a backlog. You may already have something like this for yourself—a to-do list.

Backlogs and To-Do Lists (Not so Different, You and I)

What's the difference? Visibility (and there's an app for that). At home, we use the Google Keep app for my "honey-do" and grocery-store lists. At work, we've used several tools to ensure visibility and share awareness (e.g., once read, you remove your name/picture/avatar, and when the last one is gone, everyone knows that everyone has read it, and it drops off the current list). Differing levels of security let you share appropriately with your boss, your team, and others with whom you collaborate while keeping things running smoothly in your personal life.

When it comes to your to-do list, you may have a hard time managing your backlog. In today's constantly changing marketplace and competitive landscape, you must constantly review priorities, so you

---

[15] https://youtu.be/8NPzLBSBzPI

apply your limited resources to the most important work. The reality is that the stuff at the bottom of your list should never get done; otherwise, you're "running too rich" with your resources. Saying "no" is something that most of us need to become more comfortable with, if for no other reason than to maintain a healthy work-life balance.

Recommendation: If you are a senior leader, you likely use a to-do list, and it may be on paper. Consider moving to a shared electronic approach for visibility or even for delegation or notification opportunities.

When we think about work, especially when working with others, it is best to have some visual representation of that work. If we look at Agile teams, they almost always use cards (usually three-by-five cards) that carry the name of the "story" and information about that "story," such as the relative complexity or size of the work, priority, blockers, assignment, dependencies, etc. Those cards then are put on a board (frequently a magnetic whiteboard), enabling them to be categorized and moved to different parts of the board depending on their status. This lets the whole team and all stakeholders see where the work is, what's in queue, etc. On a recurring basis (based on what the team has agreed upon), a review of the cards in the "backlog" is performed to confirm/update priority or anything else that may have changed since the last review, also known as backlog management or backlog grooming. As work is completed, those cards are moved to "Done," and card(s) are pulled from the backlog and moved into active status. This "review and update" is how we make sure the team is working on the right work (the highest priority for which they have the prerequisites and sufficient capacity to complete in the current iteration).

Agile—Thinking in New Ways, Iterating, Being Cool, and Collaborating

In February 2001, a group of seventeen software developers got together to share ideas about a new approach to building software. The serial approach, frequently called "waterfall," was (arguably) effective, but no one loved it. It took too long, rarely resulted in what the customer wanted or needed, and was painful for all. These developers knew that if they could talk with the users, collaborate on and embrace evolving designs, and uncover hidden needs and expectations, they could be more efficient.

The "Agile Manifesto"[16] was the result of this retreat, and the world hasn't been the same since. They were not the first folks to feel this way, but their Manifesto caught on.

> Jack: As a Lotus Notes developer without formal software development training (self-taught Visual Basic developer, and unrepentant hacker), I never thought to take a serial approach. With the WYSYWYG (What You See is What You Get, more or less) visual user interface of Lotus Notes, we started with what the application should look like—data presentation, user interaction, etc.—in our first meeting (user experience). As a developer, I could share ideas and make suggestions based on what I could do, based on what I knew about their objectives, etc. (which, as a small company, was usually a lot and didn't require too much background discussion). We could identify features and capabilities that they might not have thought of or thought too complex (like a calendar-based interface or automated workflow). Later, we'd figure out where we'd get the data, algorithms, and integrations (usually with at least one of our IBM AS/400s). This almost always resulted in delighted users, with a more feature-rich experience than they had even hoped for.

While not really Agile (no sprints, no line/team, etc.), it did address some of the basic tenets. There are multiple flavors of Agile, such as Scrum and XP (extreme programming), which I suggest you don't get too hung up on. Let's first assess where you are and what you want to do; then we'll pick and choose from a broad array of tools that will best suit you and your environment. You may be wondering why we didn't say anything about your industry or the technologies you use. They could have some impact, but that will be a secondary consideration (you'll see why as we discuss the "What" and again in the "How").

---

[16] www.agilealliance.org/agile101/the-agile-manifesto

In today's world, there is less and less need to develop software from scratch. In fact, the only time you should even consider it is if it will clearly and positively differentiate you from the competition and give you a distinct advantage. Buy, configure, and integrate should be your primary path. This doesn't hurt or help the benefit or opportunity to be Agile, or more accurately, to benefit from agile thinking.

But what do we mean by "agile thinking"? We can derive it from the principles defined by the original group of developers behind the "Agile Manifesto"[17]:

We follow these principles:
Our highest priority is to satisfy the customer
through early and continuous delivery
of valuable software.
Welcome changing requirements, even late in
development. Agile processes harness change for
the customer's competitive advantage.
Deliver working software frequently, from a
couple of weeks to a couple of months, with a
preference to the shorter timescale.
Business people and developers must work
together daily throughout the project.
Build projects around motivated individuals.
Give them the environment and support they need,
and trust them to get the job done.
The most efficient and effective method of
conveying information to and within a development
team is face-to-face conversation.
Working software is the primary measure of progress.
Agile processes promote sustainable development.
The sponsors, developers, and users should be able
to maintain a constant pace indefinitely.
Continuous attention to technical excellence
and good design enhances agility.

---

[17] http://agilemanifesto.org/principles.html

Simplicity—the art of maximizing the amount
of work not done—is essential.
The best architectures, requirements, and designs
emerge from self-organizing teams.
At regular intervals, the team reflects on how
to become more effective, then tunes and adjusts
its behavior accordingly.

These can be much more broadly applied, and many organizations have, including in hardware, data, and non-technology domains. If you substitute "results" or "deliverable" in place of software, you can apply this to the delivery of value to our customers, internal and external.

DevOps—Delivering Technology Solutions Better, Faster, and Cheaper

DevOps is likely to be the most interesting and exciting advancement in technology of our time. It builds on Lean and Agile and takes them to the next level of performance.

The meaning of DevOps has morphed from the initial definition coined by Patrick Dubois, which was getting development and operations to work better together, to something that is focused on accelerating delivery of key business capabilities to get feedback as quickly as possible.

To compete in the next decade and beyond, that is really the key problem that large enterprises need to address. How to be able to go from customer need or idea to being able to deliver something to their customers to get feedback on whether this moves the needle associated with a key business driver (e.g., selling more widgets).

Why DevOps?

Every system is perfectly designed to get the results it gets.
—W. Edwards Deming

The basic problem facing companies is how to react more quickly to meet the needs of their customers and be competitive in the marketplace. This requires a delivery system that *reduces the time from idea to customer delivery and feedback*, which we define as lead time. It is critical that an enterprise agree on this definition because history teaches us that without this type of true north to guide their activities, the system that is designed will fall short of our goal to become more responsive to the business.

An example of this is the Agile implementation in most enterprises. Agile can provide better quality and predictability. But because Agile is almost always implemented in the design/develop/test cycle of the value stream, it doesn't provide any true increase in speed of delivery. Large enterprises typically fall into a "water-scrum-fall" model, where they still do work as large projects and only go fast through development team iterations.

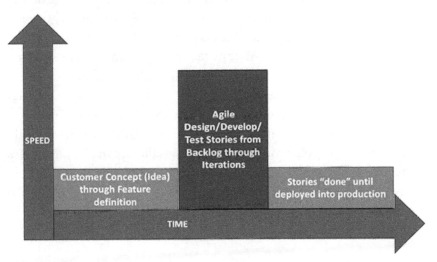

Image 1. Water-scrum-fall—"before" DevOps value flow.

As shown above, there is still a large delay in getting work to the teams, and there is also a delay in getting completed development work into production. So, while this approach is a good first step, it generally will not reduce end-to-end lead time.

> You can't directly change culture, but you can change behavior. Behavior becomes culture. — Lloyd Taylor

Cultural changes are needed to empower teams to have more

self-service and control over their delivery journey. A key cultural component is to achieve a balance between ensuring that a capability and the underlying technology can be supported for the entire enterprise. At the same time, teams must be empowered to use it in the way that best suits them to serve their business.

A good example of this relates to deployment. In the past, the model might have been to centrally govern and control how deployments were done. This created several problems. It meant that teams that needed more flexibility would be motivated to find ways outside the tooling to do what they wanted. These types of local optimizations created variations, which increased waste and inefficiency. A second problem was that the team owning the tool became a bottleneck for any type of change needed for another team's configuration. This added a service-level agreement to the process, which increased the delivery lead time and process complexity. A third problem was that any technology changes were evaluated from the basis of comparing tool A to tool B. This typically resulted in decisions primarily focused on financial costs of the tool rather than the impact of the tool on the team's ability to deliver more quickly and efficiently. The evaluation needs to be based on what value is added to the integrated delivery pipeline supporting the value stream. In some cases, there were actually disincentives built into how tool usage was internally charged back to the teams using them. This incented the team to utilize less of an automated tool to reduce the charge-back and resulted in resorting to more inefficient manual activities.

The Math of DevOps[18]

What is the value proposition of DevOps? First and foremost is the notion that DevOps is all about attaining speed to value. Speed is king right now because so many business leaders we work with are under the gun to deliver value as quickly as possible. Yet, because of the high cost of technical debt, they have come to a state where speed has to be sustainable. It's no longer easiest to go outside their organizations for

---

[18] This section comes from a blog on DevOps.com that was written by Sanjeev Sharma, Carmen DeArdo, and Lee Reid, https://devops.com/the-simple-math-of-devops/

the high-priority key projects, as mobile applications were recently done. They need a holistic approach that builds on their existing capabilities.

What does that have to do with math? Here's the thing: Everyone is trying to minimize the time it takes to deliver value and attain feedback. We can think of the time to delivery as the following equation:

$$T_{DELIVERY} = T_{PLAN} + T_{DESIGN} + T_{DEVELOP} + T_{BUILD} +$$
$$T_{DEPLOY} + T_{TEST} + T_{FIX} + T_{RELEASE} + T_{EVALUATE}$$

In an optimal world, or a software factory that is fully automated, the $T_{DELIVERY}$ is optimized by minimizing the time for each of the tasks required to complete the delivery. Most organizations follow a software development life cycle (SDLC) or application lifecycle management (ALM) that is based on this simple math. They estimate the time to do each part, and then the total project plan is the sum of the parts. Further, they tend to define work in relatively large chunks or big-up-front style of work definition, which inherently increases the time for each task (T_x). As a result, the industry has about a 50 percent (or worse) failure rate when it comes to completing a project within the estimated time. That causes a lot of hardship because the business can't count on IT to deliver value to customers in the projected timeframes, let alone with speed.

Because application delivery is a set of very human-oriented tasks, a key factor that determines the speed to value is trust. When you draw out the value stream, mapping of how work gets done, the results from a lack of trust begin to emerge. As members of software delivery teams lose trust in the validity of the work as it flows through the lifecycle, a large amount of rework and waste is introduced:

$$T_{DELIVERY} = \frac{T_{PLAN} + T_{DESIGN} + T_{DEVELOP} + T_{BUILD} +}{T_{DEPLOY} + T_{TEST} + T_{FIX} + T_{RELEASE} + T_{EVALUATE}}$$
$$\text{percent TRUST (0–1)}$$

That is, the tasks we do in a delivery cycle are impacted by the degree of trust we have in the handoffs from one to another. If we have zero trust, then our $T_{DELIVERY}$ will be infinite (divide by zero). Complete trust and our $T_{DELIVERY}$ is limited only by how fast each task can be performed.

Let's use a hypothetical situation to walk through this:

On a given project team, if the plan has about a fifty-fifty chance of being right, the design is about 85 percent right, the developers get about 90 percent of the implementation right, the testers get about 90 percent of the test cases right, and the release team has about a 95 percent reliability of having the right stuff together to release, then your trust factor is something like this:

Plan 50 percent x design 85 percent x implementation 90 percent x test cases 90 percent x release 95 percent = percentage trust

(1) x.5 x.85   x.9   x.9   x.95   = percent trust

= 33 percent trust

Ouch! That's a multiplier of the time it's going to take no matter how fast we do all the delivery tasks. In other words, we're always limited by our trust factor. That multiplier comes into play with additional tasks we have to add into the equation to counterbalance the lack of trust. Then our equation becomes something like this:

$$T_{DELIVERY} = T_{PLAN} + T_{RESCOPE} + T_{DESIGN} + T_{ARCH\ REVIEW} + T_{DEVELOP} + T_{TECH\ DEBT} + T_{BUILD} + T_{REBUILD} + T_{DEPLOY} + T_{REWORK} + T_{TEST} + T_{RETEST} + T_{FIX} + T_{REFIX} + T_{RELEASE} + T_{ROLLBACK} + T_{RE\text{-}RELEASE} + T_{EVALUATE}$$

And that's the issue a lot of organizations are facing today. Too many wasteful tasks, checks, and balances have crept into our delivery process due to lack of trust.

So, how does DevOps help this problem? It's simple, really; the DevOps approach is to attack the trust issue head on while simultaneously reducing the task time (T_x) to shorten the overall time to delivery. For example, if we apply a DevOps practice of breaking work up into small chunks, getting it out to users early, and getting the feedback, we can immediately impact the overall $T_{DELIVERY}$. That's because we're positively impacting the numerator and denominator with that practice. That is, by limiting the scope we make it easier to understand; less effort-consuming to transform to working code, test, and deploy;

sooner to obtain feedback; and more likely to know if we're on the right track.

It is likewise for other practices. The key is finding the balance of what practices to apply to maximize this equation for a given organization and their current bottlenecks and wastes.

DevOps practices address speed to value, which depends upon trust, with three main impact points:

1. Clarity: a clear definition of desired outcome(s)
2. Collaboration: team-wide communication and visibility
3. Consistency: systematic and repeatable steps

When a team can master these three elements, the time to perform each task will shrink and the degree of trust will increase. DevOps practices impact these trust-building elements:

Clarity:
*   Break work up into smaller chunks and iterate
*   Seek a minimum viable product (MVP)
*   Define clear outcomes, "sponsor" users, and verify by "playing it back" (design thinking)
*   Reduce dependencies with loosely-coupled architectures (containers, micro-services, SOA)

Collaboration:
*   Form cross-functional teams (end-to-end)
*   Use big visual information radiators
*   Have a "single source of truth" for all development assets—requirements, code, deployable assets, infrastructure as code, etc.
*   Be transparent with metrics
*   Plan and reprioritize frequently
*   Actively seek user feedback

Consistency
*   Automate, automate, automate
*   Continually improve by replacing manual tasks with automation

Speed to value will be enabled by eliminating those bottlenecks and waste that have developed due to lack of trust. The key for organizations is to recognize that the current practices are maxed out and not sustainable when trying to move at higher speed. Try using this simple math to help organizations understand how to move ahead and how solutions can be applied to attain speed to value.

Implementing practices that improve delivery require a culture in which groups and teams are positioned to deliver better and more quickly. Just to be clear, these are not all IT practices (e.g., MVP or Minimum Viable Product is the domain of leadership and product owners). Once these true cultural issues have been addressed, the organization can successfully reduce lead time and creating a more efficient delivery-value stream and a foundation of underlying technology that reduces overall costs and improves quality.

But wait, there's more!

This evaluation of efficiency and technology looks at how much time it takes to get work done and points to improvement options and opportunities. DevOps poses a cultural challenge: some aspects of it run counter to engineering principles that many of us learned with respect to capacity and response time, as well as "bundling like work" to gain efficiencies.[19]

> Carmen: When I worked at Bell Labs, we would apply queuing theory to determine how best to package information to send it across the network. A basic premise revolved around a tradeoff between throughput and response time. On the one hand, the more messages that were packed into the packet, the more the payload would improve capacity because the overhead of processing the packet of information would be spread across the messages. However, waiting to accumulate enough call processing information meant that the packets would be transmitted less frequently, increasing the response time.

---

[19] This section draws heavily from a series of blog posts written by Sanjeev Sharma, Carmen DeArdo, and Lee Reid that were published on DevOps.com see https://devops.com/the-calculus-of-devops/

A simple example of this is making trips to the grocery store. If one wanted to spend the least amount of resources (time, gas, car wear, etc.) on shopping, then one would make less frequent trips and buy larger amounts of food. So, if the Smith family made one trip a month and spent two hours, then their average time per week spent on shopping would be thirty minutes. If the Jones family went every week and spent an hour, then they would be spending twice the time and four times the gas on grocery shopping. However, if the Smith family ran out of an item (say, cereal), they would have to wait, on average, two weeks before it was replenished. The Jones family average on any item that they ran out of would be 3.5 days, in comparison.

So, when the 2014 DevOps report was published,[20] stating that areas that deploy more frequently get customer feedback more quickly, that was expected. However, it wasn't expected that these organizations also have higher productivity. So exactly what is happening here that seems to be in basic conflict to the principles of throughput and response time?

Keeping Up with the Joneses

If we think of a pre-DevOps state for a medium to large enterprise, it may be typical for applications to be released (deployed into production) only a few times a year to provide business functionality. (Perhaps there are more frequent releases for "unplanned work," like defects and other changes or operational work.) For the sake of this discussion, let's call this the Smith Application. So, from a business perspective, the business wants to pack as much work into the Smith releases as possible given they have only a few cracks a year at getting new business functionality into production.

Smith Application Characteristics

- It delivers business value three times a year (every four months).
- Cost is C1.
- Business Value (BV) delivered is V1.

---

[20] "2014 State of DevOps Reports," Puppet Labs, IT Revolution, https://puppetlabs.com/sites/default/files/2014-state-of-devops-report.pdf

- Average time from concept (e.g., story) being ready to be pulled from the backlog to the time it is delivered to the customer is two months, plus any additional wait times (e.g., prioritization).
- BV delivered per year is 3*V1.
- Cost per year is 3*C1.

Now let's transport over to the Jones Planet, where the application is released into production with new business capabilities at the end of every two-week iteration. In this case, the business is more concerned with providing a constant demand flow into IT than they are with debating over whether a given feature/story will be included in this particular release. Instead, there is a constant prioritization (or continuous planning) process that ensures the highest-value work is being fed into the IT pipeline.

Jones Application Characteristics

- It delivers business value (BV) twenty-six times a year (every two weeks).
- Cost is C2.
- BV delivered is V2.
- Average time from concept (e.g., story) being ready to be pulled from the backlog to the time it is delivered to the customer is one week, plus any additional wait times.
- BV delivered per year is 26*V2.
- Cost per year is 26*C2.

Based on the previous engineering analysis, we would expect the following:

1. Smith annual cost (3C1) < Jones annual cost (26C2).
2. Smith annual BV (3V1) > Jones annual BV (26V2).

So, the tradeoff (we would believe) Jones is making by delivering more frequently is that they are spending more money and are delivering less business value on an annual basis.

However, the data from the previously referenced DevOps report is just the opposite. In fact, the findings are that enterprises that deploy smaller units of work more frequently have much higher quality and much higher productivity (capacity). So, what's going on here?

A New Paradigm

If you go up to any IT team (even an Agile one) and ask them why they don't deploy business value more frequently, they will generally refer to the following types of wait states of waste that they encounter:

- Waiting for work (lack of consistent flow)
- Waiting for somebody else to do something (dependencies from other teams)
- Waiting for environments (contention)

One major root cause of this is the dependencies that arise when large enterprises pack a lot of work into infrequent releases. From a planning perspective, the process is elongated due to prioritization discussions, because being on the wrong side of the line can mean a months-long delay in delivering a product to a customer. Ask a business-portfolio leader what their highest priority is for IT. I am guessing they'll be able to tell you in a matter of seconds. However, most large organizations can spend several months a year planning their annual portfolio of IT work. Some organizations spend more than 50 percent of their new project build time prior to a single story entering an Agile development team's backlog!

As we saw earlier, much of an organization's success depends on trust. One trust factor is clarity, which speaks to understanding the changes that each release brings to the IT and customer environments. Therefore, a factor that works against trust is the notion of delivering more things less frequently. Better controlling change is therefore a good notion.

> Trust is inversely proportional to the number of dependencies in a release.

There is another hidden component of waste associated with "big bang" initiatives. Let's return to our grocery example. Chances are that the Smith monthly excursion results in buying some stuff they end up not using. Perishable items are not spread out very well when they aren't purchased more frequently. Likewise, in IT planning, we tend to put a bunch of stuff in our IT delivery basket that we don't know for sure we will need, and we end up with a lot of wasted effort for features hardly used or needed. Some enterprise estimates are that 50–65 percent of what they put into large releases does not actually result in true value to the business. Doing more frequent releases allows a constant discovery process to better guide the usage of IT resources on what is truly of value.

> Waste is proportional to the size of a release.

In other words,

> Yield (value per IT investment) is proportional to the frequency of releases.

Revisiting the Math

If we revisit the earlier model, with the addition of trust, we come up with the following equation:

$$T_{DELIVERY} = \frac{T_{PLAN} + T_{DESIGN} + T_{DEVELOP} + T_{BUILD} + T_{DEPLOY} + T_{TEST} + T_{FIX} + T_{RELEASE} + T_{EVALUATE}}{percent\ TRUST\ (0-1)}$$

here are increased costs associated with having larger and less frequent releases in medium/large enterprises.

- Planning cost T_{PLAN}
- Development complexity $T_{DESIGN} + T_{DEVELOP} + T_{BUILD}$
- Testing complexity T_{TEST}
- Release and change-management complexity $T_{RELEASE} + T_{DEPLOY} + T_{EVALUATE}$

Trust percentage: Even if everything was proportional between the Jones and Smith models, the component of trust that impacts clarity, consistency, and collaboration is much lower for large (Smith) releases. Given that trust has a multiplicative impact, this alone accounts for the results found in the studies.

While one clearly needs to be sensitive to the changes they are introducing into the business, the ability of business stakeholders to pull capability when they want it and have it available more frequently is not only good for customers but also has extreme benefits from an IT perspective, in terms of increased productivity and reduction of technical debt. The challenge is to convince leaders in both the business and IT areas of the merits of more continuous planning and frequent deliveries. Unicorns may have led the way in this type of thinking, but it is actually the horses that will benefit most from this type of cultural shift, because it is the horses[21] that have the most to gain in mitigating the dependency factor, which can undermine quality, productivity, and cycle times.

Delivering Better

We've promised not just faster and cheaper but also better. Let's look at that for a minute.

What we hear many times when discussing DevOps with areas is "Yes, but ..." such as,

- But we will impact security
- But we will impact availability
- But we will impact audits

To be successful, we need to turn these into a "Yes, and..."

- And we can improve security by automation of scanning earlier in the life cycle

---

[21] "The Phoenix Project," Gene Kim, Kevin Behr, George Spafford, http://www.amazon.com/The-Phoenix-Project-Helping-Business/dp/0988262592

- And we can improve availability by reducing MTTR (mean time to release) and releasing work in smaller batches
- And we can improve audits by having more visibility in changes at every step in the process and automating the collection of this information

There was much discussion at the recent DevOps Enterprise Summit[22] conference about providing more industry guidance for areas like audits. Many enterprises who are implementing DevOps practices are running into roadblocks due to the process, expecting the same type of evidence that has been collected in the past presented in the same manner. Topo Pol and Jennifer Bradley gave a brilliant talk at DOES17[23] in which Topo spoke about how we have turned certain roles into "button pushers" to achieve separation of concerns.

The Problem: Who Approved That Code Submission?

As bottlenecks are addressed and the speed of delivery increases, it becomes more evident that the current processes implemented by compliance organizations (e.g., audit and legal) will surface as challenges to moving more quickly. A great example of this is separation of duties. In general, duties are separated to protect against somebody being able to write code, approve it into the code repository, and then deploy it to both test and production environments. Because this does not provide any checks and balances, this will generally create a finding from an internal (or external) audit team and need to be addressed.

One method of addressing this is to ensure that the person writing the code (the developer) is not permitted to approve this code being accepted into the repository. Using a capability like pull requests (supported by tooling like GitHub), one can configure the tooling to ensure that the developer of any code in the pull request is not permitted to approve this being accepted into the repository.

A policy that could be adopted and configured into the tooling as

---

[22] https://events.itrevolution.com/us/
[23] https://www.youtube.com/watch?v=Fs_uYIbxrw8

a persistent pattern might look like this: If Jane writes the code, then another person (Paul) has to review before it can be accepted into the code base. If Paul then writes code later, Jane or perhaps another person working on the team or application (Joan) can approve it. In this way, nobody is ever allowed to approve their own change into the system.

Implementing this process, one might think they have addressed the above concern. Well, as Lee Corso[24] might say, "Not so fast!" Discussions with auditors have revealed that even if this policy is adopted and documented, it might not be enough to avoid a finding from an external auditor. Why? Because the external interpretation of separation of duties might be that only people who do not have the ability to create changes can have approval rights. So, in my example above, if Paul is approving code submissions, then Paul can never write code.

This stricter interpretation is the same type of mindset that led us to the original problem that DevOps was created to address, namely, the case where teams wrote code and threw it over the wall to the ops team to support. The people who are most qualified to review and accept the change are the people who know the "most," not the "least," about the development being done on this system. Therefore, basically creating a separate group of "approvers" from "developers" is not only wasteful, but it also leads to less effective reviews.

Another Problem: Who Approved That Change into Production?

A key DevOps practice is automation throughout the delivery pipeline, from code commit through the certification of the code release into production. The criteria for certifying the tests that must be passed to release code into production is a QA (quality assurance) function. In the past, most of this was done manually either through manual tests or at least through a manual check that the tests have all passed, which typically included areas such as

- Unit testing
- Integration testing

---

[24] https://en.wikipedia.org/wiki/Lee_Corso

- System testing
- Security testing
- Performance testing
- User Acceptance testing

A last step in this process was then the formal documentation of a change request that needed to be approved as evidence of the scope of the work being done and approved prior to deployment into production.

As these tests and results are automated and certified, it is now possible to for the entire activity starting with a code commit to be automated through deployment into production, which can include the automated creation and approval of the change request.

Given the fact that this type of process can be configured into the delivery pipeline in a way to ensure that the developer of the code, the approver of the code, and the creation of the certification criteria are all unique for this change, one might again think this meets the needs of compliance. However, because many auditors have been trained to look for the person who approved the change, they may not be satisfied with an automated, machine-generated approval process. In one discussion with an auditor, they were very clear that there needed to be a single individual who could be blamed in the case of a finding (the "one throat to choke"). Since machines have yet to be jailed (although HAL in *2001: A Space Odyssey*[25] did suffer some consequences when he uttered, "I'm sorry, Dave. I can't do this"), the automated solution described above may still be met with some resistance.

The Solution

A good way to address compliance situations is to avoid waiting until the end of the process or an audit to address this. Instead, organizations should implement Gene Kim's "Second Way"[26] of amplifying feedback loops. In this case, start the feedback early even when a policy is going to

---

[25] https://en.wikipedia.org/wiki/2001:_A_Space_Odyssey_(film)
[26] "The Phoenix Project," Gene Kim, Kevin Behr, George Spafford, http://www.amazon.com/The-Phoenix-Project-Helping-Business/dp/0988262592

be written. Include compliance in this process to ensure their input and concerns are addressed in such a way that implementing this policy still allows for effective delivery, including the automated approval of code into production.

The next step is to build this pattern into the pipeline tooling to ensure that any team using this tooling will automatically meet the criteria of the policy and thus the needs of compliance. This also motivates teams to adopt tooling that will make the enterprise more consistent and efficient across their value stream.

Moving Mindsets

As we continue our DevOps journey, it's necessary to move mindsets to think about different ways to solve these problems. Everyone in the company needs to think about how they are supporting the goal of being more responsive to business needs. Reducing lead time and deploying more frequently can't just be the focus of the IT delivery teams. Optimizing the delivery value stream must become the focus of the entire organization, and that means it must be part of our core values, or our *culture*.

That's what we'll look at next, the culture of the organization and how we can lever organizational design to support and sustain the different future to which we aspire.

Start with the Basics—Concepts and Foundation

Who Are We?—Cultural Alignment

Tell me what you care about; better still—how you show it with your actions, your wallet, and with your goals and ambitions.

Let's write a story about your organization. Where did we come from, and how did we get here? Let's tell the story of you. Start by describing some times when *who you are* was demonstrated by *what you did*.

When we ask someone who they are and what they do, we usually get a manufactured answer. Rather, we get to learn this by understanding what they do, what they think about, and where they spend their time, effort, and money. Just like Mom used to say, "Actions speak louder than words." Or as US President John Kennedy said, "What you do speaks so loudly that I cannot hear what you say" (he was paraphrasing Emerson)[27].

Stories are the best way to collect, store, and share information. It was true at the dawn of history, and it's still true. A good story also encapsulates a lot of information that is otherwise lost, such as the atmosphere, the feelings, and multitude of perceptions from different perspectives, cultural aspects, and impacts. Stories are more engaging and easier to follow and remember. Have you read *The Phoenix Project: A Novel about IT, DevOps, and Helping Your Business Win*? If not, you should. We'll be referencing it throughout this book as well. It is informative and easy to read, due in no small part because it is told in story form.

But let's get back to the story of your organization. What are the primary influences in the culture? Who are the leaders, and what do they stand for? Tell the stories of the victories won and the battles lost. Tell us about the glory days, and if there were tough times, what were (are) they like? What does the ideal future look like? The story of your organization paints the picture of your culture.

The leadership of an organization has a lot to do with the culture, or the lack of an intentional culture. Strong, authentic leaders inspire, drive, and lead. Such leaders include Sir Richard Branson, Jack Welch, and Elon Musk. They might not always be right, but no one can doubt who they are and what they stand for. No one likes a "phony baloney" because we can't trust them. There's no basis for us to assume that what they say is true or that there really is a benefit *to me*. If we aspire to truly lead, we must be authentic. If we want to inspire, then we have to be ready, willing, and able to choose the hard right over the expedient not-right and lead "from the front." It's a "hearts-and-minds" thing.

Leadership comes in many flavors. This isn't a topic we'll address here except to say it will be one of the most powerful influences on your culture and how your associates will behave.

> Jack: One of the most colorful and dynamic leaders I've ever had the pleasure to work with engendered a safe environment for his team with his policy of "kick up

---
[27] https://quoteinvestigator.com/2011/01/27/what-you-do-speaks/

and kiss down" and his self-described job of being "a human crap shield" for his folks. A West Point graduate and McKinsey alumni, Mike Figliuolo has a lot to share with you. Check out his blog and leadership content at www.thoughtLEADERSllc.com. You'll be glad you did, and so will your team!

Establishing a successful strategy requires an understanding of your culture and how it came to be. Authenticity is the key to successful alignment. Without a strong and direct connection between who we are and our goals, there is little chance of a sustainable transition. Sadly, this is why most weight loss doesn't last; the diet and exercise programs don't stick because they aren't part of our fabric. When it does become a part of who we are, it sticks.

> Culture eats strategy for breakfast.
>
> —Peter Drucker

While there may be some debate as to whether Mr. Drucker actually said this, there is not a lot of debate regarding its truth.[28]

Understanding our current culture

First, you have to know what the current culture actually is (not just the leader's view of what they want it to be) before assessing whether it is feasible to actually change it.

Many things have changed during our lifetime, and often the change was due to technology. Perhaps the biggest loss has been civility and respect for people. Many would suggest that this trend started long before social media came along, but it certainly hasn't helped. Our culture does many things for us; one of them is to provide a foundation for how we think and behave.[29] This is important to us on both the macro and micro level.

---

[28] https://www.forbes.com/sites/andrewcave/2017/11/09/culture-eats-strategy-for-breakfast-so-whats-for-lunch/#6d656ccd7e0f
[29] https://thedecisionlab.com/culture-affects-work/

Carmen: At the 2017 InterConnect conference, the DevOps track was filled with discussions about cool technology and the ways companies are using them to improve their delivery capability. But a common thread in many talks involved changing culture, which is critical to any successful transformation. Often, a question was asked: How can we affect the mindsets of folks who are working in "legacy" areas, like mainframe, or in roles like manual testing or performing manual infrastructure tasks?

As I reflected on this question, my thoughts turned to something I had learned from listening to a previous boss, Tom Paider, and his cohort Mike Orzen (authors of *The Lean IT Field Guide*),[30] talk about the 4 Ps of lean: purpose, problem-solving, productivity, and people. Tom and Mike always stressed that lean starts with "respect for people." Without that, any type of transformation is futile.

So, my answer to the question posed above was "How are you investing in the people whose mindset you want to affect?" While it's great to talk about accelerating delivery, deploying in the cloud, and automation techniques, if the message is that this only applies for some areas or people, then others are going to feel left behind. Therefore, the message needs to be that if you really want to change culture and affect people's mindset, you need to demonstrate that you are invested in all of your associates and willing to help them develop the skills they need to be a part of the transformation.

One of the reasons I reject the notion of "two-speed IT" or digital-only transformations is that I believe (as do many others, like IBM Distinguished Engineer Rosalind Radcliffe) that DevOps principles and

---

[30] https://www.amazon.com/Lean-Field-Guide-Roadmap-Transformation/dp/1498730388

practices apply to all types of development, including mainframe. Are you including legacy teams as part of your Agile or DevOps transformations? Are you allowing teams to "opt out" because of certain characteristics of the work that they are doing?

Applying DevOps practices to packaged solution deployments, mainframe applications, and distributed systems of engagement matters because everyone needs to deliver everything more quickly and because a sense of inclusion builds a workforce of people better primed to move as needed. You can also keep everyone engaged in a DevOps-centric environment by holding internal tech conferences where employees teach each other about various tracks and where experienced IT workers are paired with less experienced ones, who can share their respective knowledge about legacy systems, on the one hand, and new integrated development environment and dev skills, on the other. An approach that has withstood the test of time is the apprentice-journeyman-master model of inclusion and development. Paired programming along with mentoring programs further this and help translate into everyday ways that foster a caring environment and build trust through relationship building and shared experiences.

A message of investment in all members will pay dividends in changing the overall culture. This type of investment not only provides valuable learning opportunities for associates but demonstrates the kind of investment and respect for people that is essential to making the positive cultural impacts needed for a DevOps or any large transformation.

> Jack: I have personally witnessed this in multiple organizations I've been a part of, most glaringly after an acquisition by another company. After the army, I joined Borg Warner. I really loved the people and the culture; they were like family. Then GE bought us. After a year, I'd had enough. I joined another company that I truly loved, LNP Engineering Plastics. They were owned by the British conglomerate ICI when I joined, but they were okay and largely left us alone. After a few years, we were bought by Kawasaki Steel, and that ended up being really good. When GE came along and was courting us

(again), I knew it was time to find my "next." Acquisition or substantial leadership changes (especially from outside the organization) often result in a new strategy or attempt to change the culture of an organization without addressing the underlying basis for how an organization acts and why. Kawasaki and the lean culture suited us very well. It really fit how we thought and operated. That was a very positive acquisition, and it did well. The GE one happened shortly after I left, and by all reports, there were many tears.

When not an acquisition, frequently this is attributed (generally not positively) to something like "Oh, great. Old So-and-So <insert leader's name here> just read a book." If we have this kind of response to our attempt to change our culture, we really need to dig deep into ourselves and double down on our commitment. Likely, we have a perceived history of making changes that haven't rung true.

If and when we have a major change, such as an acquisition of an organization or a reorganization of our own team, how do we treat the people that will be affected? How do we maintain an environment of respecting and caring for people who are not going to be a part of the team? How do we communicate to those who will be a part of the team about the future and let them know that not everyone will be moving forward with us?

One organization we know of committed to keeping a strong associate base and limiting the tenure of contractors while also limiting the number of contractors and vendors; it resulted in more impact than expected. Some of those contractors had deep expertise and knowledge that wasn't transferable (organizational impact) and associates lost friends and team members who had worked with them for years (personal impact). In this case, these decisions, like many others, were not made lightly but were vital to the health and long-term viability of the organization. These are real "wounds" that must be treated with great care and respect to heal well.

Understanding why we act as we do and identifying the underpinnings must be the first step on our journey to changing our actions. Our behaviors across the spectrum of our interactions must be consistent and signal our intent and commitment to any "new normal."

Like a weight-loss program or any other life-changing behavior modification, feasibility is generally within our control to the extent that we can actually change ourselves. For most of us, the probability of ceasing to be is enough, but that isn't always the case. We must be realistic about what we can change, how much we can change ourselves, and how much change the environment will support and sustain. "Walking the walk" is so much more important than "talking the talk," so planning and executing authentic demonstrations that are highly visible is critical.

Structure and Process

If an organization needs to become faster to respond to changes in technology or the marketplace, heavyweight processes and a hierarchical structure will make us less nimble. Of course, the larger and more entrenched an organization is to "how we used to do it," the more difficult and painful the process will be. There are multiple strategies to accomplish this kind of change, and many have done so effectively. One example is General Electric. Over the years, they have embraced new concepts, sometimes almost to the point of being "a religion" such as their adoption of Six Sigma in the 1990s. Their focus on process control drove significant changes and made them much more formidable in the markets in which they participated. They demonstrated improved quality, lower costs, and better focus on priorities.[31] [32]

More recently, organizational structure has been at the forefront, making organizations more responsive to the market and driving innovation (which has become the most important differentiator in today's marketplace). "Flattening" the organization or removing layers between the senior leadership and workers, has driven out cost and improved communications. But this too isn't without some challenges, specifically

---

[31] https://www.6sigma.us/ge/six-sigma-case-study-general-electric/

[32] https://www.brighthubpm.com/change-management/69148-the-story-of-six-sigma-and-ge/

around how we view our work and accountability.[33] In his book *The Tipping Point*"[34], Malcolm Gladwell looks at this phenomenon at Gore Associates (of Gore-Tex °fame), which follows the "Rule of 150." This "rule" says that 150 is the maximum number of people a group can have for that group to function efficiently. It is an extension of research and experience around organizational effectiveness that all supports people's capacity for direct communication and interaction. There is a large body of research and experiential data that supports organizational structure and design, and, not surprisingly, there is a lot of conflicting ideas and theories regarding what is optimal or even feasible, not to mention competing priorities of simplicity (flattening) and complexity (matrixed).[35]

Most importantly, create your structure in a way that truly empowers and supports your teams. As part of your organization's transformation into the digital powerhouse it can be, you will likely be shifting or redefining your culture. This a time when you can really make a difference that will truly reset your course. Eliminate the turf wars, the political empires, and the overgrown kingdoms that set up over time[36]. Break free from what has been holding you back. Empower your teams and send the message that must be embraced: We are more than we have been because we choose to multiply our resources; we are not merely additive with our thinking. We will walk the walk and prove that one plus one equals more than two. Show your people that you care for and believe in them, and give them the flexibility and power to be their best. They will rise to the occasion and will surprise themselves and you (not really, because you believed in them from the start).

All this brings us to what our focal point should be—our people.

---

[33] https://www.huffingtonpost.com/zev-gotkin/corporate-hierarchy-work_b_1962345.html
[34] https://www.amazon.com/gp/product/0316346624?ie=UTF8_and_tag=ideacon-20 and linkCode=as2 and camp=1789 and creative=9325 and creativeASIN=0316346624
[35] https://hbr.org/2011/02/the-importance-of-organization?gclid=CjwKCAjwnLjVBR AdEiwAKSGPI8AcJtPMPuXFjv3jcAfuaDIJbiCeY1Vga29IKrt4AugxVETQaIbY2hoC6 bYQAvD_BwE
[36] https://hbr.org/2011/02/the-importance-of-organization

People

It is almost a trite truism that our people are our greatest resource. But sometimes our structures and processes tell another story. US President Theodore Roosevelt famously said, "People don't care how much you know until they know how much you care."[37] I think that's true, and I bet you do too.

Having the right people in place is critical. Having the wrong people in place is usually fatal. The real trick is to know which is which. This is what separates great leaders from managers. Hiring good people is hard for some, but I've found one core truth: hire on character. You can teach skills, but character cannot be taught in the workplace.

There are many theories and competing ideas of how to surround yourself with the right people, but for my money, there are a few key indicators of whom you want on your team:[38]

- They help you identify your blind spots and make you a better leader.
- They are multidimensional and understand how your business operates from different perspectives. A technology person who doesn't understand the market has limited value.
- They are multipliers—natural team builders who know how to scale and grow their resources. They see or find synergies that make 1 + 1 equal more than 2.
- They show up for the rest of the team and make others in the organization feel important. A "win" for one at the expense of another isn't a win at all. This is a team event. Collaboration isn't just nice to have; it is essential and non-negotiable.
- They don't rest on their laurels. They are lifelong learners who are not only pushing themselves but those around them to be better, grow stronger, and challenge everything. Hire people who are smarter than you.

---

[37] http://www.doseofleadership.com/20-inspirational-theodore-roosevelt-quotes/
[38] https://www.bizjournals.com/bizjournals/how-to/growth-strategies/2017/12/five-signs-you-have-the-right-people-on-your-team.html

Making sure you've got the right leadership team in place is essential. But for all but the smallest of organizations (who don't need this kind of structure), you also need to communicate with the rest of the organization.

In their book *Made to Stick*[39] Chip and Dan Heath dig into a great mystery: "Why do some ideas thrive while others die?" Along with Gladwell, the Heath brothers look at recent history, decompose the questions, and derive answers that help us craft and deliver messages that captivate our intended audiences. "Stickiness" is the propensity for a message to be heard, remembered, and then shared. There are six common characteristics to sticky messages:

1. It is simple.
2. It is unexpected.
3. It is concrete.
4. It is credible.
5. It is emotional.
6. It's a good story.

Is there a recurring theme here? There sure is: *the story*. Good stories are powerful.

Organizational change management (OCM) is critical. There are many models to choose from, each with its own advantages and disadvantages. Some of the more popular ones include Lewin's change-management model [40] (unfreeze, change, refreeze), McKinsey's 7S Framework [41] (strategy, structure, systems, shared values, style, staff, skills), and Prosci's ADKAR model [42] (awareness, desire, knowledge, ability, reinforcement).

We encourage you to leverage one of these, or any other OCM approach, and commit resources to your advantage. Getting these foundations in place will go a long way toward making your changes successful and long-lasting.

---

[39] http://heathbrothers.com/books/made-to-stick/
[40] https://www.mindtools.com/pages/article/newPPM_94.htm
[41] https://www.mckinsey.com/business-functions/strategy-and-corporate-finance/our-insights/enduring-ideas-the-7-s-framework
[42] https://www.prosci.com/adkar

Incentives

Sometimes we forget that altruism isn't the strongest of incentives, and while self-actualization may be at the top of Maslow's hierarchy, there are several other needs that must be satisfied first.[43]

Indeed, even as Jack Welch transformed GE with Six Sigma, part of the "magic" was incentivizing people to change their behaviors. While he absolutely provided strong leadership, training, and the resources to support the implementation, just as importantly, he tied promotions and bonuses to the attainment of Six Sigma goals.[44]

A critical part of the ADKAR model, and any attempt at meaningful change, is helping those who must make the changes understand "what's in it for me?" It may seem a little crass at first, but it's the most effective tool in our toolbox for getting folks to "buy in and sign on." In some cases, it can be as simple as "The company gets to stay in business, and therefore you get to keep your job." But this runs thin quickly, and the result may just be that the individual decides to find a job with more security.

In an article for the Society for Human Resource Management called "Cash vs. Non-Cash Rewards,"[45] Diane Cardrain lays out a compelling argument against the use of money as an incentive, at least as the main or only way of rewarding higher performance or encouraging desired behaviors. In fact, the use of cash can backfire and turn into perceived "entitlements" that result in undesired behaviors, or it may become an expectation that, if unfulfilled, becomes dis-incentivizing. There can also be a diminishment or "tarnish" when tax or other implications are realized.

> A soldier will fight long and hard for a bit of colored ribbon.
> —Napoleon Bonaparte

A modern corollary to Napoleon might be "Developers love stickers."[46] Sometimes, an earnest "thank you" or a bit of public recognition is all that's

---

[43] https://en.wikipedia.org/wiki/Maslow%27s_hierarchy_of_needs

[44] https://www.6sigma.us/ge/six-sigma-case-study-general-electric/

[45] https://www.shrm.org/hr-today/news/hr-magazine/pages/0403cadrain.aspx

[46] https://www.fastcompany.com/3015764/sticker-styling-14-laptop-covers-from-tech-innovators

wanted or needed. The key is ensuring that there is a clear connection between the desired behavior or outcome and the reward. Understanding what is valued and treasured also points to a personal connection, letting everyone know that leadership is in touch with those who are delivering.

> Jack: For example, at a plastics company I worked at for many years, the workers had hard, dirty jobs in demanding conditions. The good news was that business was good, and there was as much overtime to be worked as workers wanted. Sometimes there was too much overtime. So paying a bonus for extra time worked became less attractive, and paid time off became the most desired reward. An expense-paid weekend away at Atlantic City with a wife, girlfriend, or family was almost heaven after working in a hot, dirty plant all week. And the employee also got to be the "big winner" at work *and* at home!

One organization we know of rewards behavior and results across the enterprise with "Bravo" awards. Another in the past used "I Got Caught" awards (it was a good kind of "caught"). In both cases, anyone could submit anyone else's name for an award, and the award notification took the form of a certificate that could be printed and proudly displayed on a team board or cube wall. The managers of those recognized were also notified of the award. A "public" thank-you that can also be put into your file for your next performance review goes a long way!

Changing and Enforcing Controls

It's tempting to say that change is a constant today, but the reality is that change is increasing in frequency and amplitude. Increasing the amount of feedback and accelerating the collection and processing of feedback is becoming the cornerstone of competitiveness. In the book *The Phoenix Project*, Gene Kim and crew talk about "The Three Ways"[47]:

---

[47] https://www.amazon.com/Phoenix-Project-DevOps-Helping-Business/dp/0988262592

1. Apply systems thinking to create work flow
2. Shorten and amplify feedback loops
3. Create a culture of experimentation and learning

We have already touched on culture lightly, and we'll dig into flow shortly, when we get into process design and implementation. For now, let's talk about feedback loops. Increasingly, our survival in the marketplace depends on learning from our performance, especially from mistakes (ours and competitors), and using the lessons learned to change incentives, resources, people, methods and processes, and other factors to foster strategic and operating goals.

Let's make sure we're on the same page regarding the definition of "feedback." SnapSurveys.com offers a definition as well as an explanation of why they think it is so important:

> The term "feedback" is used to describe the helpful information or criticism about prior action or behavior from an individual, communicated to another individual (or a group) who can use that information to adjust and improve current and future actions and behaviors.
>
> Feedback occurs when an environment reacts to an action or behavior. For example, "customer feedback" is the buyers' reaction to a company's products, services, or policies; and "employee performance feedback" is the employees' reaction to feedback from their manager— the exchange of information involves both performance expected and performance exhibited.
>
> Who would dispute the idea that feedback is a good thing? All can benefit from feedback. Both common sense and research make it clear—feedback and opportunities to use that feedback helps to improve and enhance, whether an individual, group, business, business unit, company, or organization—and that information can be used to make better informed decisions. It also allows us to build and maintain communication with others.

Effective feedback, both positive and negative, is very helpful. Feedback is valuable information that will be used to make important decisions. Top performing companies are top performing companies because they consistently search for ways to make their best even better. For top performing companies "continuous improvement" is not just a showy catchphrase. It's a true focus based on feedback from across the entire organization—customers, clients, employees, suppliers, vendors, and stakeholders. Top performing companies are not only good at accepting feedback, they deliberately ask for feedback. And they know that feedback is helpful only when it highlights weaknesses as well as strengths. [48]

Getting feedback, especially when it is directed at how we can do better, is a gift! In her article "Feedback Is a Gift: Seven Tips for Giving Feedback to Others," Carole Robin at Stanford[49] reminds us just how precious this gift can be. Unvarnished feedback is something that we can never get alone, and we should give and get it as freely and graciously as we possibly can. Feedback should be treated as though it were the most precious of our resources, because it is. Decisions that do not include the lessons learned from feedback are dangerous and should be avoided at almost any cost. There are multiple channels and opportunities for feedback, and we should exercise as many as completely as we can.

Consumers today expect frequent updates and new features, and those expectations extend to business consumers as well. The statistics of feature releases are amazing today, with Amazon averaging 23,000 releases per day, Google 5,500, and Netflix more than 500[50]! DevOps is how this is happening—it may be the reason you are here in the first place.

Automation and systems tools are critical components of our continuously online world and are basic expectations of our customers today.

---

[48] https://www.snapsurveys.com/blog/5-reasons-feedback-important/
[49] https://www.gsb.stanford.edu/insights/carole-robin-feedback-gift
[50] Per Infoworld.com "Devops: Farewell to major software releases and welcome to transparent software", 12 June 2017

System monitoring, and the alignment and enforcement of controls on our processes, should include automated and out-of-band collections to the maximum possible extent. These range from focus groups to continuous real-time monitoring of systems using tools like New Relic and other automated application performance monitoring (APM) tools to continuously monitor environment, server, and application performance. Effective controls should be implemented that enable immediate corrective action as well as ongoing analysis that can uncover opportunities for improvement. Detecting performance issues prior to customer realization and applying corrective action before performance degrades to sub-standard levels should be the objective of systems monitoring, controls, and communication (notification).

What Do We Do? Understanding Work

Work—Motion Study, and effectiveness

As we launch the real Information Revolution, we can take some macro lessons with us from the Industrial Revolution. We are steeped in our history, and we need to continually challenge the status quo both to evolve and keep pace with the changing environment capabilities and needs. Leveraging the things about us that make us different *and* better makes sense, as long as it is also rooted in our relevant value proposition. We do, however need to make sure it is still relevant, or we run the risk of being the world's best buggy whip manufacturer.

While Lean and Agile are currently trendy, they are in fact not all that new conceptually; they provide solid foundations for getting from where we are to where we need to be.

But do we reject and throw away the lessons from our past? Of course not! We need to reevaluate and choose the pertinent pieces and reapply them in the context of today's challenges, issues, and opportunities. For example, Henry Ford and those who studied time-motion and distributed work processes provided a basis that would become Lean, when the Allies helped Japan rebuild after WW2 and a byproduct was the Toyota Production System. But to be clear, this is not just a manufacturing play, not by a long shot!

The movie *The Founder*[51] has a pivotal scene in which the McDonald brothers and their team choreograph their processes. They find the best way to work together by enabling each role to be optimized within the operations of the whole team. They started with a "non-collision" approach and then optimized each role across the value stream without allowing a local optimization to reduce collective performance. They measured the result in output and time without any compromise in quality.

Watch them apply Lean concepts in this scene from the movie [52]

So, what is the "special sauce" that drove McDonald's internally and their success in the marketplace? It has been the relentless pursuit of continuous improvement—speed, consistency, waste elimination.

> Jack: When I was a salesman peddling plastic, the sea of stainless steel in every McDonalds was my siren. When I walked through the labs at the headquarters building to meet with engineers, it was the focus on consistency that struck me the most. It wasn't just that the same amount of ketchup and mustard were applied; it was the timing and the exact location of the application. They still like stainless steel. Oh, well.

Effectiveness must be attained before efficiency should be attempted, as efficiency without effectiveness is worse than pointless; it accelerates waste.

For this part of our discussion we're going to focus on planned work. Later, we'll talk more about planned work (and break it down into external, internal, and operational) as well as unplanned work and neglected work.

---

[51] https://www.imdb.com/title/tt4276820/
[52] https://www.youtube.com/watch?v=u00S-hCnmFY

Standard Work: Brush and Floss Only the Teeth You Want to Keep

Standard work is a concept that has been around for a very long time. So why is it that we don't see more of it? First, what is standard work?

There are two flavors:

Process → What→	What do we do that makes us different, that creates value?
Role → Who→	Who does that work? Who can help make it happen faster and better?

Role Standard Work: Outlines what is expected of someone in that job.

Process Standard Work: Details the way we accomplish the work, who is involved, what tools are needed, what are the inputs that are necessary, what repeatable steps result in a predictable (and desired) output.

When we look to the manufacturing world, we do see a lot of standard work. We see it in many service fields too. In many cases, it is necessary because of thin profit margins and low tolerance for error. But so far in the "business" world, we don't see it as much, for reasons that tend to be self-serving or flat-out wrong. What are some of those reasons? Let's take a look so we can knock them down, and then we'll look at some compelling reasons why we need to start using standard work for everything that we care about.

Reasons given for not doing standard work:

- It's too complicated
  - No, it may take some help at first to start to decompose it, but even putting a man on the moon could be broken down into the individual steps needed.

- It requires my "specialness"
  - It can be scary at first, and this is why the culture needs to be addressed up front. For most companies, this is quickly becoming necessary to survive. People need to understand

that the intent is not to replace but to enable improvement and realize higher value.

- It's too much work
  - It seems like that initially; however, depending on several factors, including the size and complexity of the organization and work execution, there may be automated tools that can simplify the initial collection and creation, as well as ongoing maintenance as improvements are made.

- There's no return on that investment of time and effort
  - Generally, this is not true (if it truly were, then buying this book would be a waste of time and money).

Every time you execute the improved processes, you will get a return based on the time × value of the improvement, plus a significant savings on new associate on-boarding for your organization.

There are seven reasons that we want (need!) standard work:

1. Establishes and documents the currently known "best way" to accomplish work
2. Provides the baseline against which improvements can be compared (measured)
3. Improves understanding and helps set appropriate expectations for results/outcomes
4. Cultivates an open culture of sharing and trust through transparency
5. Reduces errors and waste by driving consistency, which also increases speed of execution
6. Drives predictability and enables measurement for improvement quantification
7. Clarifies communication of expectations and basis for associate on-boarding/training

We don't need (or want!) to document every single process that happens, just the ones that are important to who we are and what we do.

What Is It That Makes You Different?

Your competitive advantage is likely directly tied to your strengths.

The approach of StrengthsFinder[53] is to focus on your strengths and make them even stronger. When we're good at something, we usually like to dig in. But we can reconsider that later. For now, we want to get even better at our core strengths.

How do you know what your strengths are as an organization or from a product perspective? For starters, a SWOT analysis (strengths, weaknesses, opportunities, and threats) can help to identify where you should focus your attention. For each category, list as many examples as you can of each in your assessment. Once you have them, prioritize them based on impact and ability to mitigate or enhance each.

Strengths	Weaknesses
Opportunities	Threats

Table 1—SWOT Analysis

How can you verify? How do you know where you stand?

Gartner is perhaps the most widely used benchmarking and analysis organization. They can help you take a hard look at how your IT organization performs versus other organizations. Looking from your own perspective is tempting, and you should start with what you know. But it is even more important to get an objective opinion. If you're not in the IT business (we'll sidestep the idea that everyone is in the IT business these days), it might be tougher to do. But there are some key benchmarks regarding your business performance, such as revenue, growth, and profitability,[54] and with a bit of market research, you can build a case for where you stand versus your competitors. After that, you'll want to take a look at

---

[53] https://www.amazon.com/StrengthsFinder-2-0-Tom-Rath/dp/159562015X
[54] https://blog.marketresearch.com/the-top-6-strategic-benchmarks

the entries in your SWOT and begin to evaluate how those compare with your organizational goals, strategic plans, and organizational definitions.

If you are in a leadership role, you need to tackle these questions before you can even start to unleash the power within your organization:

- For the things that you are good at, how closely aligned are these with your core mission?
- How about your culture, do they align or support it?
- Do you have clearly documented processes, policies, and procedures to ensure consistent understanding and application?
- How are new associates trained or made aware of these?

You do not need to document everything, and please don't try. Just like my dentist likes to say "Only brush and floss the ones you want to keep." Simplicity is the key to doing this well.

This is probably a good time to take a look at what you do, all of it. What could you not be doing? What should you not be doing? Who is doing what? Should they be doing that? Prune and thin as you take a hard look at this. Focus.

As you look at the things that differentiate you from the rest of the pack, you need to dig into each of them by looking at where you can accentuate your strengths. Perhaps you need to develop some new strength to either counteract or mitigate your weaknesses. Opportunities should be considered, such as where you can focus significant resources to solidify your position or counteract competitors and market pressures.

As your strengths, weaknesses, opportunities, and threats are visualized, confirmed, and evaluated for impact, you may need to reconsider your priorities and adjust your plans. What of these are the most important to you and your strategic direction? Do any of these change or shift your strategies? If not, why not?

You don't have to be great at everything; in fact, you don't even have to do everything. In today's highly specialized and interconnected world, outsourcing non-competitive advantage capabilities can give you the best position of cost, flexibility and, staying at the forefront of best practices.

WorkDay [55] *and Guidewire*[56]: These enterprise software vendors/ products are case studies in commoditizing what we used to think we had to do for ourselves, by outsourcing the tools while focusing on your people, maintaining currency, and jettisoning old baggage (outdated processes, ineffective or bad policies, harmful or illegal practices). It used to be that we built and maintained our own software. Human resource software has been a "packaged solution" for a long time, but companies still had to maintain it in their own data centers. WorkDay[53] takes away the need the commit your own resources to keeping it running and current and offers a cloud solution that enables you to focus on the other parts of your business that differentiate you from your competition. Similarly, GuideWire[54] lets insurance companies focus on their differentiation, not on industry-standard best practices in policy management, claims management, and billing.

The things that you do, and the processes that you rely on that are not part of your core competencies, not a strategic capability, or are not a differentiator that give you a competitive advantage are the first target for outsourcing or utilizing a shared (commercial) service.

Shu-Ha-Ri: Where Are You on Your Journey?

Shu-ha-ri roughly translates to "to keep, to fall, to break away."

- *shu* (守) "protect," "obey"; traditional wisdom; learning fundamentals, techniques, heuristics, proverbs
- Apprentice

Everyone has their "first day," and when we look back retrospectively, we usually see just how painfully naive and unskilled we actually were. At first, we don't know what we don't know.

This approach is a typical skill development path. In the beginning, the initiate, or apprentice, blindly follows the teachings of the teacher. Basic mastery is the goal, and there are clear "right" and "wrong" ways of

---

[55] https://www.workday.com/en-us/homepage.html
[56] https://www.guidewire.com/

doing things. The most wise (rare at this stage) are humble and strive to learn. They "sit at the feet" of those who do know, or at least they think they do, to see and learn. We make the big and small mistakes and learn how to recognize which is which. We become familiar with the tools and learn the skill, improving our ability to select the appropriate tools based on the situation or desired results. We generally begin with the simplest of tasks, work, and projects. Then, with time, we become competent and are reasonably able to accomplish basic tasks and begin to appreciate the finer points. This is the journey of the apprentice. Many will continue this path to become fully competent and able to accomplish every task necessary to be considered fully capable and a professional in their chosen field. Once he or she has mastered the basic skills, the competent practitioner may move to the next level with significant practice and experience.

- *ha* (破) "detach," "digress"; breaking with tradition; detachment from the illusions of self, fully skilled, aware of limitations and capabilities
- Journeyman

As we gain experience, we begin to understand just how little we actually know in the bigger scheme. While our mastery of the basics is demonstrable, the attainment of full mastery of these basics leads us to realize we've only scratched the surface. We learn more complicated and intricate patterns and approaches. We begin to appreciate how the simplest tasks have the opportunity for far more graceful accomplishment than the rough attempts and successes we've realized. We may even see how and why we had to move through that "phase" to get to a higher level. This "journeyman" level is where most will spend the majority of their life or career, placing higher importance on other aspects of their lives. The carpenter who is also a musician or magician, or the plumber who devotes his time and energy to the care of animals—these are worthy pursuits that are for the greater good and self-fulfillment, to be sure, but they distract one from reaching the highest levels of the domain.

In the second level, the competent practitioner knows the basics and has truly mastered the subject. At this point, they also know when and how to reinterpret the rules and be flexible within the spirit of the rules and fluent with the practices. This journeyman represents the majority of fully-skilled practicing professionals. But a few will find the calling to take their skill, understanding, and development of their craft to the highest level.

- *ri* (離) "leave," "separate"; transcendence; no techniques or proverbs, all moves are natural, becoming one with spirit alone without clinging to forms; transcending the physical
- Master

The highest level, the master craftsman, or guru is at the top of the food chain. The master makes the rules, and the master sees the limitations of the rules and the next level beyond the current practices. What really distinguishes the master is vision. The true master understands if, when, and how the rules need to evolve or be completely replaced.

In the development of our work processes, and even more so, in the development of our workers, to understand where we are on this journey, we must know where we are on the continuum of these levels of skill.

We must provide the culture that supports and rewards the cultivation of these skills and empower them to provide the highest level of value possible. Sometimes, this means not promoting them into roles for which they cannot be happy, satisfied, or successful. A good doer rarely makes a good manager or leader.

II. WHAT

How Are We Structured and How Do We Act?

Sun Tsu, George Patton, and Bruce Lee walk into a bar …

Strategy, tactics, and operations: we need all three, and they must be coordinated and planned together. How we are structured as an organization will have profound effects on our culture, the way we think about our work and how we accomplish it, and, ultimately, whether we'll be successful or not.

Our organizations are frequently structured based on functions or capabilities. We typically have finance and accounting, sales and marketing, engineering, manufacturing, etc. This does a lot of good things, including ensuring that we have development and oversight from groups that have more skilled and experienced resources. These can share and grow the more junior associates. There are also core competencies for each role that must be maintained at a minimum level, but ideally these are grown. But do we really need to structure our organizations in this way to accomplish that? No. There are many ways to address this, such as internal centers of excellence (COEs) or communities of practices, which are usually internal groups. External groups typically have more diversity in skill types and experience and may offer greater access to new ideas. Organizations such as PMI[57] (the Project Management Institute), IEEE[58] (Institute of Electrical and Electronics Engineers), and the AMA[59] (American Medical Association) offer depth and breadth of experience, resources, and broadly accepted practices. A key consideration here must be where these practices fall within the core competencies and compet-

---

[57] https://www.pmi.org
[58] https://www.ieee.org
[59] https://www.ama-assn.org

itive landscape of your business. Depending on what you truly are good at, these approaches can keep you grounded with generally accepted practices and standards. This is where the apprentice can learn a great deal about commonly accepted practices and behaviors and a journeyman can get a broader view of other thoughts and trends. Be aware of their role and propensity/capability to be at the forefront of new ideas and improved practices. Where these fall in your world as competitive advantage versus commodity should be a strong guide for you.

Specialization versus cross-skilling is one of the considerations we should wrestle to the ground. In many ways, having a solid understanding of multiple domains can be very helpful. Cross-skilling can significantly improve outcomes, for example, when a product-development team has clear understanding of the market and production capabilities. In most cases where this is vital, we address it via cross-functional teams. Additionally, many organizations drive this via "rotational" roles, especially among leaders or incoming associates. A challenge in these cases is keeping the knowledge current and relevant to the needs at hand over time.

A matrixed approach to getting things done is far more prevalent than it was twenty-five years ago. Sometimes this is a permanent structure, but far more often, it is a temporary assignment based on a project or initiative. If an organization keeps "spinning up" new matrixed teams as each new project comes along, it does so at the risk of never really allowing those teams to become proficient as a team. Certainly, there are times when the work is temporary. Perhaps we have a lot of variability in what needs to be done, making a "standing" team inappropriate. You will need to take a hard look at what you are doing, and this might mean rationalizing what you do, depending on the nature of your business. However, when we look at your "core," we should find many more similarities than differences every time. For most organizations, this is the most common model, where functional organization is predominant, and projects are subordinate and provide resources on an assignment basis:

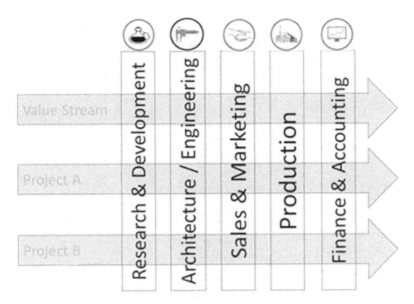

Image 2. Vertical or functional organization.

We also should design our associate development plans to address the capability and need for strategic, tactical, and operational views of our work, our planning, and our execution. (You do have associate development plans, right? These are not to be confused with annual performance evaluations; they're not even related.) This is very challenging, as typically it is difficult to assess if someone has particular aptitude for such work and to recognize their capability, particularly if it is outside your own expertise.

We're not done with this topic yet, but we'll come back to it after we talk about work execution. We'll consider how our organizational structure can help (or hinder) how we think about work and how we can drive the flow of value through more quickly by organizing appropriately. But as a preview, this is where we should be headed:

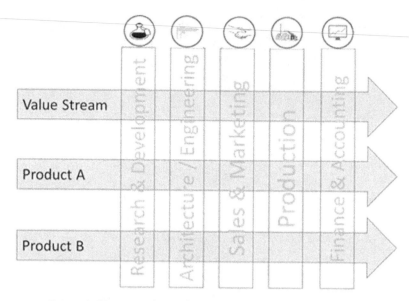

Image 3. Horizontal or value stream/product organization.

In this model, the value stream(s) or products are the primary construct, and the capabilities are more loosely coupled to provide guidance and technical support. In this construct, the ideal is that the head of these capabilities is the *ri*, or master craftsman, for that domain.

Making It Work, like Really Work

So, how and where do we get started? (Oh, and by the way, we still have our day jobs to do, and we need to keep it flowing.) First, you have to take a hard look at what we do and how we do it. We're probably really, really good at a few things, reasonably good at a few more, and mediocre (or worse) many things. It's so much easier to get to the top of the hill than to stay there. We have to do better to stay at the top of the hill, even better than what got us to the top of our current hill. We can feel the breath of the competition on the back of our necks. We also must realize that what got us here is not necessarily going to get us to where we need to be. This is especially true in today's world, where there are crumbling barriers to entry into any and every market, with technology driving most of that.

Many companies are realizing themselves as a technology company that happens to serve whatever markets in which they participate. We worked with a Fortune 500 company that came to this conclusion, and decided they needed to change their approach to technology to avoid disruption. So, we took a "snapshot" of how they were working to build and deploy technology solutions. We captured the current work from the time the business said, "We need this" to the point where it was deployed into production. We broke the flow of work (or value stream) down into "segments" (an intentionally vague word). We then wrote a brief description of the result of the activities, processes, and work products that led to a specific result or outcome, like "define requirements," "develop the architectural approach," or "build the solution."

Then we announced a "Hackathon," where we invited everyone in the organization to pick a segment, build a self-forming team, and sign up to spend a day (a *long* day) together to share their solutions with everyone, including how they took the current processes to the next evolutionary level. We encouraged teams to create a theme for their topic and to wear costumes. The result was amazing! Teams gathered from all around the company; we used teleconferencing systems and reserved conference rooms with telepresence equipment at all our major locations.

Between the time when the teams signed up on our SharePoint site—to identify team members, their "day job," and the "segment" they were going to tackle—and the day of the event, we reminded them to "fall in love with their problem." We urged them to gather their own thoughts and ideas, and, as a team, to consider what they really wanted to "fix."

In preparation for the event, we encouraged team to get ready by thinking about their chosen topic by ensuring they had thought about their problem from every perspective. This was fairly easy for the groups, since they were working on something that they do every day! We asked them to (1) *immerse* themselves in the problem that they wanted to improve and then to (2) *frame* the problem into a single idea that would realize the biggest impact or improvement.

We did a quick workshop first thing in the morning (along with using arts and crafts supplies to make team signs, flags, banners, and posters to identify themselves and their "topic") and started an innovation mindset using this model, to begin:

Jack's Focused Improvement 4F model[60]:

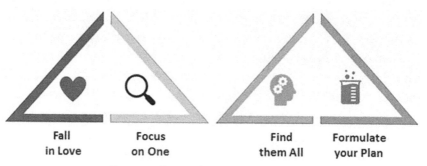

| Fall in Love | Focus on One | Find them All | Formulate your Plan |

Image 4. Focused Improvement model.

When people arrived in the morning, we gave them stickers that they would use to represent their approval on work, tools, or processes that they could recognize as "theirs" later on, as well as name tags with their name, team, and role printed on them. We pointed them at tables loaded with craft supplies and then supplied lots of coffee, bagels, and donuts.

For our "kick off," we went over our "worksheet" for each team, which outlined the components of the solution—the inputs their part needed, the resources necessary (people, tools), and the output they would produce. Then we had each team introduce themselves and their theme, and we had a contest for their themes and the corresponding sign/banner/flag. This enabled the other participants to identify and later find the teams with which they had to interact. For each process, they had to get an "endorsement" from someone who had that "role," and for each input, they had to ensure that it was still available from an upstream process. Similarly, they had to ensure that any change to their output would still meet the needs of any downstream process. These endorsements were demonstrated with the stickers that were given with each name badge. The results looked like this:

---

[60] In the appendix of this book, you will find a more in-depth presentation and discussion of the Focused Improvement 4F model/process. Jack also does a workshop on this process for teams or organizations for implementation as a standalone innovation process or as part of a line/team retrospective. You can also learn more at https://FocusedImprovement.us.

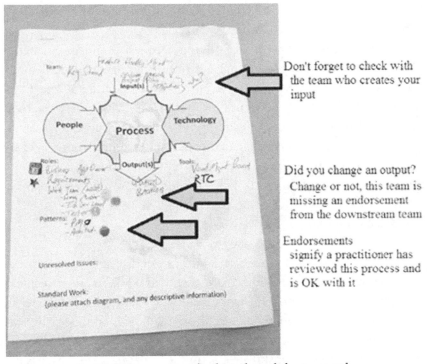

Don't forget to check with the team who creates your input

Did you change an output? Change or not, this team is missing an endorsement from the downstream team

Endorsements signify a practitioner has reviewed this process and is OK with it

Image 5. Process Standard Work worksheet example.

The endorsement collection was the most fun for a lot of teams, finding the right folks, collaborating on their solutions, and sometimes meeting new people in jobs/groups they had never heard of!

We then asked each team to draw a simple flow chart of the steps in the process. Of course, some teams didn't get that far. Occasionally a team didn't actually solve the problem, or solved the wrong problem. Sometimes they didn't actually even solve any problem, other than what to do with free and plentiful coffee, soda, pizza and Chipotle. ☺ All good.

The results were amazing, beyond even our most optimistic dreams. We had literally hundreds of deeply-engaged associates who had an investment in the outcome and wanted to see their work make a difference.

My team then took all of this information and saved every bit of it on our SharePoint® site. We then engaged small teams of thought-leader practitioners to help us comb through this mountain of data to help us make sure we had connected all the dots. We filled in the gaps where there was a missing link and curated the results into our first cut at our process standard work.

Next was the hard work of building a cohesive end-to-end series of processes that would form the basis of our next-generation delivery processes. In many cases, we replaced the Word document and Excel spreadsheets that had been in use for many years with enterprise tools that provided many benefits, including version control, security, distributed access, and enabled automated processes ranging from workflow approvals to automated processing, such as the creation of a work item for a line backlog automatically from a defect uncovered in testing.

Process Standard Work

The goal of each piece of process standard work is a clear and concise description that every team follows to execute their work. In our implementation, we don't cover how the work is done but rather the "what, when (sequence), and what tools". In our culture the how is addressed by part of our culture, which includes "Capability Leaders." These are led by the "gurus" of that domain or skill group, the "Ri's" of our earlier discussion. By separating the "what" from the "how," we add some "future proofing" to our processes and also enable teams that may have specialized capabilities or needs to address those locally. By keeping the other components consistent, we enable more flexibility for teams and resources to move across the organization with the ability to recognize the work patterns and processes, even with some "local flavor" or evolution.

Each piece of process standard work has the same elements, with a goal of being as short and simple as possible:

1. Purpose—a single sentence that describes the expected outcome or value of this work
2. Scope—a single sentence that outlines the components of the work to be done
3. Capabilities—a list of the skills necessary for this work (e.g., architect, user experience designer, security engineer, developer, tester, scrum master, project manager)

4. Inputs—a list of documents, pre-conditions, information needed (e.g., story, test case, requirement, architectural design)
5. Outputs—a list of the expected results of the work
6. Guidance or references—job aides, instructions, additional explanations of upstream and downstream processes, other background or execution detail, or resource descriptions. In some cases, it can be very helpful to include who has what kind of responsibility, such as:
    i.   Accountable—who guides or approves the work?
    ii. Responsible—who actually does the work?
    iii. Consulted—what is the required input and consultation?
    iv. Informed—who needs to know the result?

    This is especially helpful when teams are adopting new processes and when new members join a team.
7. Process Flow diagram —a picture that shows the work steps and any input/output/mid-stream process loops or other pictorial means of describing the work and the way it is accomplished
8. General work steps a step-by-step list of the steps and actions executed
9. Metrics—how we will measure the results and attain them
10. Patterns, fitness for purpose, and techniques

For organizations that have a lot of repetitive and/or widely divergent work within the same construct, or are CMMI' oriented, this section can provide information to help guide teams with those concerns or opportunities. Examples would include any pre-determined auxiliary or ancillary processes that may need to be invoked or involved depending on the specifics of the work to be executed. This is particularly helpful for maintaining consistency of process when the work at hand may be very different, such as implementation of a COTS (commercial off-the-shelf) software solution versus a custom coded solution, or a hardware/software combination solution, such as a firewall.

Role Standard Work

Start with the existing job description. Most companies have a job description including at least enough information to post a job ad in the newspaper or on an online job board.

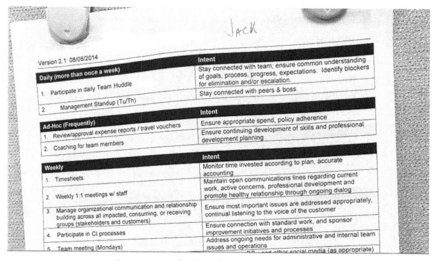

Image 6. Role Standard Work example.

Depending on the size and formality of your organization, this can be done at a global level, where the expectations of everyone in a particular role are the same, such as for a purchasing agent or material handler. In other organizations, it may be handled at an individual level, particularly when associates "wear multiple hats" and have responsibilities spanning multiple roles.

Whichever approach you take, the basics are the same. What are the things that are done, the frequency with which they should be executed, and why are they done (what's the value).

The Role Standard Work should list everything that is expected of someone, ranging from daily to weekly, monthly, quarterly, and even annual tasks. There are multiple reasons for doing this and benefits that result.

Templates and worksheets for Role and Process Standard Work can be downloaded at www.DeterministicProcessDesign.com

Clear Expectations

When Gallup° does their survey and measures the engagement of associates within an organization, the most basic or fundamental question is "Do I know what is expected of me?" [61] When expectations are unclear, setting goals and understanding how those goals align with organizational needs is impossible.

> Jack: One way we can drive clarity and prepare for full automation of our processes across the entire value stream is to ensure that our process design is deterministic. This is a relatively new concept, something that I have developed with a lot of trial and error over the past fifteen years. The concept grew out of my master's degree program research project using artificial intelligence, using an inference engine for a practical application with polymer selection at LNP Engineering Plastics. If you would like more information on this topic, look for an upcoming work entitled "Deterministic Process Design: The Secret Sauce", at www.DeterministicProcessDesign.com.

Deterministic Process Modeling and Automation

> *In mathematics, computer science, and physics, a deterministic system is a system in which no randomness is involved in the development of future states of the system. A deterministic model will thus always produce the same output from a given starting condition or initial state.* [62]

As we design our processes, it is important to keep our true objectives in mind. Certainly, clarity of the process documentation is necessary, but our larger goals are to design the processes in a way that it leverages

---

[61] http://news.gallup.com/businessjournal/186164/employees-don-know-expected-work.aspx

[62] https://en.wikipedia.org/wiki/Deterministic_system

consistency of process with the ability of the practitioners to utilize their capabilities to the fullest. A practitioner from another team should be able to recognize the activity and contribute to the outcome nearly immediately, even if their "home team" does it slightly differently. Enabling and empowering team members to be creative and apply their uniqueness and insights is truly where art and science blend.

Empowerment and Ownership

Having a dialogue about the role between the associate and their supervisor/manager/leader is one of the most important aspects of your culture. Being clear about expectations and making it personal sets the stage for empowerment and ownership of the work. At first, the work may be uncomfortable for both. However, the message that it sends—"You are a professional and I trust you to do it well"—is empowering. Sure, there will be issues and shortfalls, and expectations will fail to be met. However, there will be an opportunity to build a relationship of trust when we focus on the result and not the person. When we accept and acknowledge the substandard result or effort and make corrective action a clear expectation and allow for growth, we create a culture where people will not only deliver but rise to newer heights and become better associates. Engagement becomes a powerful driver that connects associates to their work, helping them become aligned with the mission of their team.

A regular review of Role Standard Work between an associate and their supervisor also facilitates an ongoing dialogue about performance. As conditions in the business, market, or an employee's capabilities change, the standard work may be updated and expectations re-synchronized. At a higher level, cross-linking the roles and work in Process Standard Work ensures that there are clear expectations and no "misses" when it comes to who should be doing what. Particularly if we are in a matrixed environment, maintaining clarity of execution and prioritizing different kinds of work (such as day-to-day work along with project or special assignment work) helps ensure consistency of expectations across organizational and work-based structures (e.g., projects).

Using Interlocking Fields of Fire

When soldiers in the field are preparing their defensive positions, whether for a night encampment or for a longer-term emplacement, they map out the area for which they will be responsible. They then coordinate their plan with the person or unit that is on either side of them. The idea is that by having a clear understanding and establishing a bit of overlap, they can be sure that there are no "holes" in their defenses.

We can do the same thing by analyzing the work that we need to do and making sure that we have every piece "covered." We can do this systemically by mapping all our Process Standard Work to Role Standard Work. Where we do not have a direct mapping, we have a gap; here, it is somewhere between probable and certainty that it will get missed.

Breaking the Cycle of Dependency

While technology is an important component of DevOps and accelerating delivery, other aspects of process and culture are critical to realizing the goal of reducing lead time to become more responsive to business needs.

If you go to most Agile teams and ask them what is stopping them from going faster, they will typically respond that they are waiting for "something." Something can include

- Work to enter their backlog
- Environments
- Another development team to provide some service or capability that is needed.
- Obstacles that need to be overcome, including:
  o Large batch sizes
  o Lack of continuous flow of work into Agile teams' backlogs
  o Calendar-based gated releases
  o Test environment complexities
  o Environment availability

When teams deliver system releases only a few times a year, the business believes they need to pack everything they can think of into that release, since waiting for the next release incurs a delay of months. This leads to large, complex releases with many dependencies. This, in turn, slows down the development and testing of these releases and requires a lot of release coordination. This results in long lead times and the inability to release frequently. All these additions compound, quickly spiraling.

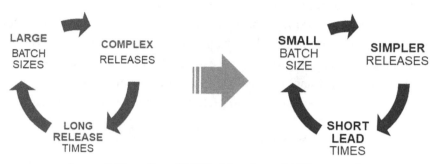

Image 7. Move from SLOW old cycles to FAST new cycles.

Dependencies are friction to accelerating delivery and come in many forms, including monolithic architectures, large batch sizes, dependent services, and test environments. One measure of how effective a team is at mitigating or eliminating dependencies is their ability to release independently. This was a key point made in the latest "State of DevOps" report.[63]

So, what are the countermeasures needed to break this cycle? They include the following:

- Smaller batch sizes
- Architectural, design, and development decoupling techniques
- Increased automation
- Readiness-based release capability

Smaller batch sizes require applying MVP (minimum viable product) techniques. When IT gains the trust of the business to deliver more frequently, the business will be more open to focus on the minimal product set of highest-priority items that they believe can deliver business

---

[63] https://puppet.com/resources/whitepaper/state-of-devops-report

value. Accelerated delivery provides the ability to test business hypotheses and gain feedback from customers more quickly to determine what worked and what needs to be changed. These quick cycles build trust, confidence, speed, and agility. The enterprises that can turn this crank more quickly gain a huge advantage in the marketplace.

Modern web architecture techniques (e.g., micro-services and APIs), along with design techniques such as feature toggling to enable dark and canary launching allow applications to be deployed independently and with direct control of customer impacts. This increases development velocity by simplifying and reducing the lifespan for managing feature or release branches in the code base.

Increased automation combined with a move to readiness-based (or independent) releases allows application releases to be deployed when they are ready rather than waiting for calendar-based change windows. They key here is not to sacrifice quality, auditability, or security but rather to build those capabilities into your applications and delivery pipeline, requiring that those certifications be earned before an application is released.

During retrospectives, we need to ask what is stopping them from releasing independently. This will uncover blockers that need to be addressed as part of your continuous improvement journey.

As discussed previously, a key element of the journey is mindset. Mindset is also reflected on the language that we use. For example, calling something "off-release" suggests it is a bad thing to be avoided. So, does getting approval for "exceptions." If your goal is to reduce lead time to improve business responsiveness, you need to deploy more frequently, which requires the ability to do this independently.

Therefore, challenge your team to understand how to do this. Sometimes the answer is that the team didn't even consider it or think it was possible or admissible. However, in order to reach your goal, you need to embrace the thinking of Robert Kennedy: "There are those that look at things the way they are, and ask why? I dream of things that never were and ask, why not?"

Designing for Resiliency

> *Resilience: the capacity to recover quickly from difficulties; toughness.*

We can set up our processes to be resilient and evolutionary, and it's simpler than you think. It's especially effective if you have individuals and teams who are motivated and have a sense of pride and propriety in their work. Reviewing current processes collaboratively and documenting them using the process standard work is more than half the battle. The remaining points are straightforward, although not necessarily simple:

- Governance
- A common repository that is broadly accessible and has version control
- A social-media platform for discussing, supporting, evolving, and enhancing the processes (this is a *nice-to-have*)

Governance needs a new approach in most organizations. Usually we have processes that need governance for whatever reason, and it becomes a set of rules that are added on in addition to some kind of enforcement mechanism. The *right* way to do it is to design the process around the objective and then make it the smoothest and easiest path. When specific criteria must be met, a simple rules-based inference engine with table-driven criteria parameters enable constant monitoring. With data collection, you are on your way to enabling statistical process control.

The common repository is a key mechanism along with the collaboration for the documentation and evolution of the processes. The resilience comes from several related dimensions:

Collaboration

When practitioners and their teams have ownership of the work that is done and the processes themselves, they view the work and their relationship with it quite differently. Collaboration drives accountability to both the process and to the resulting work.

Commitment

> Individual commitment to a group effort—that is what
> makes a team work, a company work, a society work, a
> civilization work   —Vince Lombardi

Understanding and harnessing commitment is the key, and there are many theories and studies that have focused on this. It is a complex combination of influences, beliefs, and perceptions, but all point to an undeniable connection between commitment and outcomes. Collaboration touches on many of these from both a personal-commitment and organizational-commitment perspective. Gallup"s engagement model gives us a solid starting point with their twelve questions[64]:

1. Do you know what is expected of you at work?
2. Do you have the materials and equipment to do your work right?
3. At work, do you have the opportunity to do what you do best every day?
4. In the last seven days, have you received recognition or praise for doing good work?
5. Does your supervisor, or someone at work, seem to care about you as a person?
6. Is there someone at work who encourages your development?
7. At work, do your opinions seem to count?
8. Does the mission/purpose of your company make you feel your job is important?
9. Are your associates (fellow employees) committed to doing quality work?
10. Do you have a best friend at work?
11. In the last six months, has someone at work talked to you about your progress?
12. In the last year, have you had opportunities to learn and grow?

---

[64] https://q12.gallup.com/

None of this is rocket science, is it? If your associates are engaged in this way, will they become committed to your organization? Not necessarily, but if they are not, there's no chance at all that they will. Am I right? Actually, the answer is reciprocity. In his landmark book *Influence: The Psychology of Persuasion*[65], Robert Cialdini shares the magical, powerful tool for truly being influential without control or being manipulative. In fact, while the motivation may be questioned in some instances, we have the opportunity to engender so much more. When the reality is that it is truly an act of generosity, or, better still, the result of a relationship of mutual trust and care, we begin to build a relationship that deepens and grows.[66] We will get so much more than just a stronger team or better results.

With the teams we've built, in the organization we've crafted, growing the culture we want, now we can kick on our afterburners and really make some changes that will take our results to the next level. Who's going to stop us now?

Tools and Technology

Is there an app for that?

We're going to talk a lot about tools and technology, so let's be clear on expectations. By the time the virtual ink dries, the list will likely no longer be complete and up to date. Even with our supporting website (www.StandingOnShoulders.us), we probably still won't be able to keep it 100 percent, but we'll try. The intent here is not to endorse any particular product for any particular purpose. We'll name names and products to help facilitate understanding. Actual performance, solution evaluation, and anything else about fitness for purpose is between you and the vendor/source. There are some open-source tools that are de facto industry standards (like Git/GitHub) that we'd suggest for any organization (we use GitHub to manage the content of this book), including Jenkins and Ruby. We'll also share the names of commercial products that we're

---

[65] https://www.amazon.com/Influence-Psychology-Persuasion-Robert-Cialdini/dp/006124189X

[66] https://www.psychologytoday.com/us/blog/stronger-the-broken-places/201510/honoring-the-rule-reciprocation

aware of to help organizations leverage the relationships they already have (e.g., IBM and Computer Associates / CA Technologies).

The Integrated Pipeline

Before and beyond its central mechanism for continuous delivery of our technology, there are multiple benefits for developing an integrated pipeline, and perhaps more feature/benefits than you've considered.

Metrics

Without an integrated pipeline, it is very difficult to measure something like the end-to-end lead time—how long it takes a customer idea to be translated into work (e.g., features and stories) and then built, tested, and deployed into production. Often, the metrics being kept are also local, and the KPIs might actually lead to local optimizations rather than reductions in end-to-end lead times. A great example of this is in the KPI associated with robot utilization in the "The Goal Story":

> **"The Goal Story"**—a story about key performance indicators (KPIs), robot utilization, and keeping robots 100 percent busy.
>
> When first introduced into production environments, robots were very expensive and a very valuable resource. Plant managers, senior leaders, and owners/investors wanted to see them kept busy all the time.
>
> However, it turned out that in most environments, if robot utilization was over 35 percent, the downstream stream work couldn't keep up. So, the company was wasting money buying raw materials to keep robots busy to produce downstream inventory that couldn't be consumed in a timely manner. Thus, waste actually increased, in the form of excess intermediate inventory and resource allocation. This KPI (key performance indicator) was not aligned to "the goal" of making the company more profitable. This is a good example of local

optimization coming at the expense of the "system." The issue of utilization is something we should dig into a little more deeply.

Response Time versus Utilization Rate

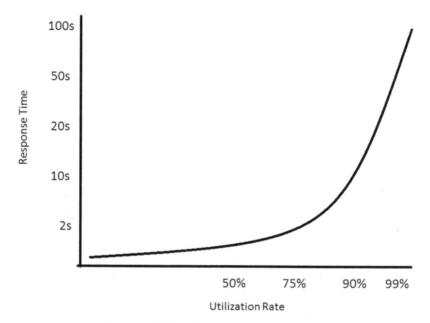

Image 8. Utilization versus response time.

This utilization versus response time graphic shows that response time (or time for getting something done) goes up dramatically when the resource (including humans) utilization increases due to too much WIP. The equation is basically as follows:

Response time = service time/ (1 - utilization).

Therefore, something with a service time of five units (e.g., seconds), has a response time of five when the resource is idle. It goes up to ten when the resource is 50 percent utilized, and up to fifty when the resource utilization reaches 90 percent and five hundred at 99 percent utilization. While we apply these concepts to machine resources (e.g. CPU and Disk) we don't apply them to Human Resources or consider the implication of allocating resources or teams at 100 percent or even 80 percent.

> Carmen: I had the pleasure of working at the local food bank not long ago. A typical activity was to load paper, packaged, and canned goods into a box, which was then loaded onto a pallet to take to the truck to deliver to local food banks. In this situation, people were assigned to stations along the conveyor belt (e.g., constructing boxes, loading cereal, paper goods, and canned goods, taping the boxes, loading them on the pallets). For whatever reason, most of the time, I ended up loading the heavier canned or jars, including applesauce. About fifteen minutes in, I would take a look up and down and line and see the following. To my left were partially-filled boxes stacking up to the ceiling! To my right were folks standing idle, looking at me to hurry up. Obviously, there was a bottleneck, and it was me! Who knew it would be the applesauce causing all these issues?

The "food bank" story is similar to "robot" example in that we don't need more boxes made (or more pallets to load completed packages onto the truck) when it's really the loading of canned/jarred/heavy goods, like applesauce, that is the constraint on the line. When you improve something to the left of a bottleneck, you create more inventory buildup before the bottleneck (boxes). When you improve something to the right/downstream of the bottleneck, you increase the idleness of downstream resources (pallets). These are local optimizations that are a form of waste. They waste money on materials, and they create more idle/waste of human resources.

Let's step back and look at this from a couple of examples.

1. *Network utilization.* Ask any network engineer about how network capacity is planned and executed. What is considered a "good" utilization rate? Depending on your ability to provision, growth rate, and specific needs, most engineers will suggest

50–70 percent. We begin to see degradation of performance and inability to manage spikes in usage. Let's consider this as we begin to design and plan for our technology architecture and design. At least the traffic is "fairly rational." Overall, we can deploy additional resources and regain necessary throughput with relative ease, so perhaps we can consider our technology landscape in the same way.

2. *Highway utilization.* Think about your drive in to work or back home at the end of the day. Do you think about the time of day and make decisions about your commute? Of course, we know that even without accidents or construction, the relatively "irrational" nature of drivers and traffic means any increase in vehicles on the road results in a decrease in throughput (i.e., it *will* take you longer to get there). Providing these kinds of resources (roads and bridges) take a lot longer and can be very disruptive. If we consider our people, processes, and culture to similarly be difficult to "provision," we should plan them a little differently.

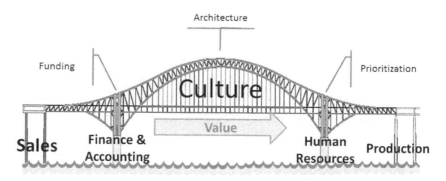

Image 9. Value-stream-supporting structures.

There are three main structural components that support the value stream (represented here as the roadway): (1) the *funding* and how it is provided, along with (2) the *prioritization* of resources and work execution, all of which is supported via (3) the *architecture* that forms the structure of the bridgeworks. All this is supported by the functional capabilities of the organization, from the sales organization that identifies and captures the intake to our value stream through the administrative elements that enable the organization to function through the delivery of the product via our production assets.

We should look at our organization and the way we operate in a holistic way, where we use the structures we put in place strategically. In this model, we can consider the supporting structures such as our functional organizational units as supporting the value stream, with our culture and the core components of *funding, prioritization,* and *architecture* of our value stream holding up. We can even take this a level deeper, by designing our value stream to support the different kinds of value that we inevitably have.

By designing our value stream flow based on its ability to be streamlined, we can use current tools that take advantage of the most advanced capabilities, while still supporting the traffic that doesn't need, or cannot take advantage of, the highest-speed capabilities we can build (legacy systems). The real beauty of this flow is that, unlike our highways, our value streams can operate in multiple dimensions.

By designing them together, we can provide maximum speed and efficiency to each one and increase safety at the same time!

> Jack: I recently attended a webinar that was presented by XebiaLabs featuring Gene Kim and Robert Stroud. They discussed building parallel pipelines based on different needs or technology paths. We could think of this as one pipeline that we use for our AWS (Amazon Web Services) or Pivotal˚ development team that is automated all the way from development (or even before) through deployment. However, we might need some manual steps for the process used to maintain the Cobol code on an old legacy application. Both, however, could benefit from multiple automation steps, such as code management (GitHub) and diverge and converge, as necessary/capable.

We have a lot to talk about regarding technology, but the most important and foundational for everything else is our integrated pipeline.

Integrated Delivery Pipeline

The DevOps Handbook[67] stresses that enterprises need a foundational pipeline in order to accelerate delivery. We believe that how you organize around this pipeline and integrate it is actually more important than the specific tools that you choose for it. There are many resources that provide information about the best-in-breed tools. Here's a small sample:

- Gartner® Magic Quadrant reports[68]
- Forrester® Reports[69]
- XebiaLabs Periodic Table of DevOps Tools[70]

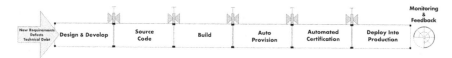

Image 10. Integrated-pipeline model.

The era of "best-in-suite" implementations is over. Organizations need to implement best-of-breed tools so that they can be easily integrated, using products like Tasktop,[71] and adapt their business processes to what the tools provide rather than falling into the trap of customization.

In the old model, companies bought into the concept of purchasing products from one or a few enterprise-approved vendors. Often, this pot was sweetened by a long-term license agreement that provided deep discounts in exchange for a multi-year commitment to using a large number of this vendor's products.

Often, this hole got bigger when the tools were customized to the "unique" needs of the business users, which typically involved buying more services from the vendor and implementing things in a way that not only made the enterprise more dependent on the vendor for upgrades but

---

[67] https://itrevolution.com/book/the-devops-handbook/
[68] https://www.gartner.com/en
[69] https://go.forrester.com/
[70] https://xebialabs.com/periodic-table-of-devops-tools/
[71] www.tasktop.com

also made it very difficult to replace these products, even when a better opportunity was available in the marketplace.

This type of process and tool "debt" causes companies to pay a heavy price when it comes to supporting tools, tracking usage, and implementing heavy vendor-relationship models. Thus, the following lessons are learned:

- Select best-in-breed tools.
- Integrate them into your tool chain using standard integration patterns and technologies.
- Use them in the way they were intended to be used (configuration is fine, but customization is a red flag).
- Utilize model-based integration so the model of workflow isn't disrupted when a different tool is implemented.

Model-Based Integration

Tasktop Integration Hub[72] is an example of a tool that allows an enterprise to model their value stream from idea to deployment and then implement integration patterns to flow artifacts and make them visible across the value stream.

When you think about the work that your delivery teams need to take on, they fall into several categories, such as,

- Business-value work
- Defects
- Technical cards

> Carmen: See my talk with Mik Kersten[73] at DevOps Enterprise Summit for more details on this.

You can see how work can then flow through agile management tools to your team in the form of changes, features, stories, or defects. Defects

---

[72] https://www.tasktop.com/product-overview
[73] https://www.youtube.com/watch?v=HrEZM1Yg7Ck

can automatically be synched into the backlog of your Agile teams to be prioritized and worked. Incidents can be turned into defects in the same way, automatically, without having to go through protracted manual activities.

As work progresses through code development, commit, and testing, the artifacts associated with these release components are visible all the way to the application of certifications for release. In this way, it is possible not only to see the work flow but also to get a true measure of end-to-end lead time.

A large advantage of having a model-based integration is that if a tool like RTC (IBM Rational Team Concert) is replaced by something else (e.g., Atlassian's Jira), the model is not changed. The new tool is simply integrated into the model through an integration pattern utilizing the vendor provided APIs. This also holds true if multiple tools are being used for the same purpose (e.g., agile life-cycle management), since all these tools can be mapped to the same model so that the flow of work is preserved (including any metrics).

Planning and Executing the Change

Assuming it is feasible, the first order of business should be to determine the approach and identify the plan for making such a change. This is a foundational strategy. Making the changes to behaviors and activities without cultural support may have short-term effects, but it will ultimately be doomed to failure. As time goes on, especially in difficult times, we'll typically revert to what we "used to do."

As we align our approach and goals with our values, we increase our ability to be sustainable. If our goals are not consistent with our current culture, we need to address the culture. Can we really change our culture? Yes, we can.

In 2011, Wharton@Work published an intriguing article, "Culture as Culprit: Four Steps to Effective Change." The author reinforces the concept of culture as critical but redirects the reader to consider that culture is both causal and dependent upon the behaviors and actions of the organization.[74] It is further asserted that a direct or single-threaded approach to changing culture will almost certainly fail. Rather, there are five pieces to this puzzle, all of which must be addressed:

- Products and projects
- Structure and process
- People
- Incentives
- Changing and enforcing controls

Projects and Products

Carmen: When I joined a Fortune 500 company in 2005, one thing that struck me was that almost all new work was organized around projects. This included large initiatives and even small enhancements. The only type of work of work that wasn't included was defects, which were typically handled by a "run" or support team.

This type of approach of doing software development was in stark contrast to my experience at Bell Labs, where work was all done in product releases except for the creation of a new type of product, which was then implemented as a project.

Some ramifications of the project approach are as follows:

- Teams go through the phases of forming, storming, and norming.[75] Frequently, when people are hitting their full stride and performing, the project ends, and the entire cycle is repeated around a new project.
- People from the impacted applications are moved to be part of a temporal project team. The entire focus is on getting the

---

[74] https://executiveeducation.wharton.upenn.edu/thought-leadership/wharton-at-work/2011/09/four-steps-culture-change

[75] See also Bruce Tuckman and his theory of group dynamics, https://en.wikipedia.org/wiki/Bruce_Tuckman.

project done in the least amount of time, using the least amount of money.
- The integrity of the existing applications that are sometimes impacted by having multiple simultaneous projects that are difficult to manage because of the project-centric focus, lack of visibility of the work being done and impacts to the application code base.
- Technical cards and defects related to the application clash with project work. Project managers have no incentive to invest in the applications being impacted or to minimize/reduce technical debt. In fact, just the opposite is usually the case: short-term thinking gets priority over longer-term sustainability when timeline and budget pressures are applied.

The figure below shows the structure where work is done by project teams impacting multiple applications. In many cases, the project manager for project A likely isn't aware of projects B and C, which are affecting the same applications as their project. The focus is on project costs and project completion rather than on frequent high-quality application releases.

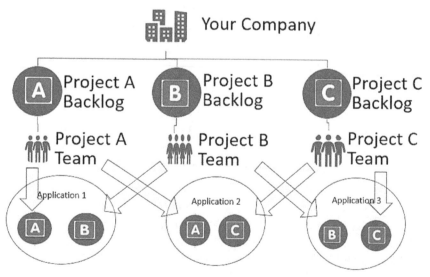

Image 11. Standard project model.

Contrast this to a product model in which work flows to established teams supporting the products. Application teams release product-related work frequently using DevOps practices,[76] including APIs/micro-services and dark launching, to mitigate dependencies. Product owners collaborate as needed to resolve priorities. Product owners invest in the applications supporting their product (e.g., tech cards/defects/risk mitigation). Product flow and dependencies are visible and managed at the level closest to the work. Teams are empowered to be as self-service as possible.

Sounds good, doesn't it? Well, let's see how this actually can be put into practice.

Here's a specific example of how work was done in the product model at Bell Labs. In the network area, there were various lines of business:

- POTS (plain old telephone service)
- Intelligent network features (things like 800 services or calling-card service, if you can remember that far back in time)
- Software-defined networks or virtual private networks used by businesses

Lines of business would have a funding stream and prioritize a list of capabilities they wanted developed as part of a rolling roadmap, with quarterly updates. These capabilities would include features that needed to be developed in network products, such as

- Switches (e.g., 4ESS, 5ESS)
- Intelligent network database systems (e.g., network control point, or NCP)
- Core network systems (e.g., signaling transfer point, or STP)
- Operation support systems

These network products had product managers who would then package features into what we would now call an MVP (minimum viable product) and prioritize them to send to the product-development team to be implemented.

---

[76] https://itrevolution.com/book/the-devops-handbook/

Because the AT&T network was built using APIs (built either on the CCS7 switching protocol[77] or BX25[78], for you die-hard techies), it was possible to implement and deploy these features independently, in what we now call "dark launching"[79] as part of today's DevOps practices. In contrast to the project model, the system-product teams stayed together and had the work sent to them rather than sending members of the product team to work on the projects. This enabled high-performing teams to more quickly implement and release these capabilities, which is exactly the model we want today to accelerate delivery and reduce lead times. The teams also supported what they built, and the team was able to release changes quickly when problems were encountered.

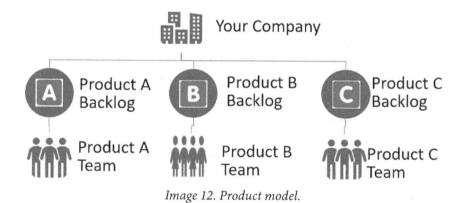

Image 12. Product model.

While this product model provides the advantages noted above, it did have some drawbacks. First, it relied on a network architecture phase that would architecture the business features based on the network APIs. Also, the releases of the products were infrequent compared to today's standards. Most products did not release new features more than once per quarter.

The model had a number of advantages:

---

[77] http://what-when-how.com/roaming-in-wireless-networks/ccs7-network-architecture/

[78] https://www.semanticscholar.org/paper/Proposed-specification-of-BX.25-link-layer-protocol-Kurshan/2e6a7c48a88360d429442d2d271bf4ed9886ee76

[79] https://itrevolution.com/book/devops-case-studies/

- It brought work to established product teams who could work independently using APIs.
- Product teams used features such as dark launching to mitigate dependences.
- Product teams did both build and run and were cross-skilled.
- Product owners regularly prioritized the product backlog.

However, it had disadvantages as well:

- It required a network architecture phase to design feature interfaces.
- It didn't use continuous delivery concepts.
- Lead times from concept to release was typically more than ninety days.

Fast-forward to the current time and organizations (e.g., unicorns, as described in the Phoenix Project[80]), which were built on single products, as Netflix or Etsy started out in the product model world. However, for large enterprises, especially those with large and diverse product or service offerings, the move away from a traditional project structure to a product-oriented structure might not be as easy. The journey may consist of various stages to move towards this type of model:

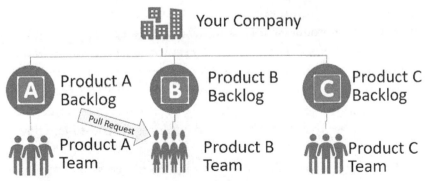

Image 13. Product model with Pull Request.

---

80 https://itrevolution.com/book/the-phoenix-project/

- Transition from moving people to the work to moving the work to established application-based teams
- Cross-skilling of application teams to be able to handle all types of work, including build and support work ("If you build it, you run it.")
- DevOps practices like APIs/microservices, feature-toggles, and dark launching to enable teams to deploy frequently and mitigate dependencies
- Inner-sourcing model using pull requests to mitigate wait states due to resource contention (more on this later)

One of the biggest differences between this model and the Bell Labs model is that in the latter, changes made to applications were done only by the product teams for which the application were part of. The network architecture phase of the project determined what APIs would be needed, and then the development and usage of those APIs were features given to the provider and consumer product teams of that capability. This required more upfront architecture work and collaboration across product priorities and resources.

Organization Structure

The integrated delivery pipeline might be the most important asset of any IT organization; however, it is rarely treated that way. Often, it is not thought of as a product at all but rather a set of disparate tools used by a specific set of users to accomplish a specific need (e.g., "create features and stories," "do continuous integration," "deploy into the cloud"). This makes it very hard not only to provide end-to-end visibility of the work-flow as described above but also to drive continuous improvement in a way that can apply systems thinking to optimize the end-to-end flow of work and activities.

Often, the support for these tools is silo-ed across organizations. These organizations are not co-located and may not even be in the same location. So, what is the correct organizational model to support the de-livery pipeline product? No matter the model that an enterprise may find itself in as its current state, there are certain activities needed to support horizontal flow through the value stream:

- Architecture
- Product ownership
- Funding
- Prioritization
- Continuous improvement

Left on their own, the vertical silos will naturally create disruption in the flow of value. Organizational and functional affinity negatively disrupts horizontal flow. Without roles that are empowered to act as true product owners and architects, which includes having funding and prioritization authority and the ability to architect improvements across the value stream, it is not possible to successfully implement and improve, or even to have, a pipeline product.

In order to reduce lead time, today's product teams need more autonomy to plan and deploy business capabilities. While APIs/microservices are still vital, when a product team needs a change to system in another product area, they need for that to happen quickly. In this case, let's assume product A in Image 13 is implementing a new capability that requires a new payment type (e.g., Apple Pay). The capability to validate that payment to a customer is provided by an application in product B. In this case, the open-source model can be applied within an enterprise (inner-sourcing). Assuming the product A team has the technical ability and expertise, they can make the changes to the application in product B and then issue a pull request to that product owner. Those owners can then review and validate the change and accept the request, including it into their application, which can be then go into their next (hopefully frequent) application release.

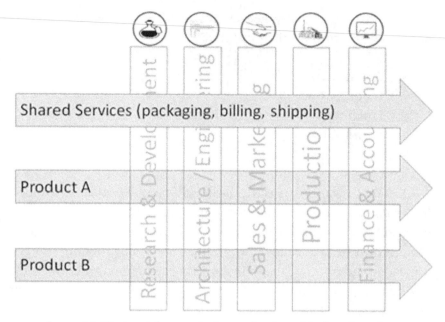

Image 14. Horizontal or product organization with shared services.

If we combine the organizational structure we discussed earlier with a product focus, we can accomplish multiple improvements. This model also layers in a shared-services model that enables non-differentiating services to be consolidated and managed more efficiently and moves those resources out of the product flow and makes them available from a "pull" perspective.

This change in approach has other organizational or role impacts as well, such as project managers. As we move to a product orientation, and especially when coupled with a shift to an Agile development model, PMs will need to move from the "PMBOK®" command-and-control approach of the past to a more nuanced role. For example, where PMs have historically planned, monitored, and in many cases directly influenced or managed the execution of the work, today that is more likely to be managed by the Agile teams and/or Scrum Masters. PMs will have the opportunity to be more strategic and to put more emphasis on managing dependencies, particularly across multiple development teams or even organizations. As organizations move into a fully operational product centric model, PMs would be candidates to move into product roles.

This model allows the time spent on status and reporting meetings to be spent doing more risk and issue management, improved organizational change management, and other tasks that typically have taken a back seat but prove to have more impact on the paying customer's satisfaction with the product produced.

Summary points:

- Moving from project to product starts with mindset move from temporal projects and short-term thinking to sustainable product longer-term thinking.
- It also requires a transformation from a centralized command-and-control (PMBOK®) project-manager centric organization into self-service self-empowered product teams.
- Utilizes DevOps practices such as APIs/microservices, continuous frequent delivery practices, including feature-toggling and dark launching.
- Mitigates delays associated with demand/capacity resource management by using an inner-sourcing model.

For more information on this topic, see Mik Kersten's book from IT Revolution: *Project to Product* at https://itrevolution.com/book/project-to-product/.

Change Preparation

Senior Leadership

Vision and resource allocation are the parts that you absolutely must lead and ensure are made visible. The culture change, shift, or reinforcements are your domain. Everyone in the organization will look to you for their cue on how to act and what to do. You must lead from the front and be authentic, consistent, and vocal. It is up to you to talk the talk and walk the walk. People must understand that whatever "this" is, it is the new normal and the expectation, or else it will become another "flavor of the week."

Success in today's world requires different leadership than we have likely had throughout our careers. Leaders who are focused on control and guiding their teams and organizations need to reconsider their roll and shift to a model that will have better results in today's culture and workforce expectations. The servant-leader approach is much more productive. Leaders who ask more questions and give their teams the leeway and resources to accomplish their missions will find that they get more innovative solutions and better results by setting the direction and then supporting their teams (and getting out of their way). This does not mean that leaders don't set standards, establish guidelines and boundaries, or hold people accountable. In my experience, every single team has risen to the occasion and has exceeded my expectations. If you're not sure about it or want to learn about it, go to www.inc.com and search for "servant leadership" or Google "why Marine officers eat last."

Set the vision, and then paint a picture of the end state or the goals so everyone can see their place in that future. Draw the boundaries and define the rules of engagement, and let everyone one know why we're doing this. Be clear about how we'll define our successes and what it will mean for the organization. Are there intermediate objectives that can help define, demonstrate, or test our progress? Give them room to maneuver and, as much as possible, the opportunity to recover from mistakes. In the army, we called this the "commander's intent."

Business Unit/Division/Department

Business

While a lot of the changes that happen involve IT (and sometimes just IT) you have a lot to do in this transformation as well. In the past, we've tended to build barriers between business users and IT, either intentionally or otherwise.

As businesspeople, we need to become more integrated with our technology partners and take a hands-on approach to getting the technology we need to be successful in the marketplace. No longer can we toss a list of requirements over the wall and then complain that we don't get what we need. Our IT partners *want* to give us what we need, and they want to do it as quickly as possible. They get it that the market doesn't wait. So, how do we do this? Go talk with them! Seriously. It used to be that business and IT spoke different languages. Not so not anymore. Let's take another look at our interactions to see if we can improve communication and, most importantly, increase the number of, shorten, and amplify feedback loops.

Secondly, let's take another look at what we communicate. In most organizations, money and access to resources are severely restricted. As a result, when someone gets to the head of the line for IT resources, they ask for everything they need or think they might want for the foreseeable future. We can change this way of thinking by breaking the work into smaller pieces (ideally at the MVP, or minimum-viable-product, level) which will help get work through the system much more quickly.

If you rely on a bus to get to work in the morning and home in the afternoon, there are only two buses each day, and you miss the first bus, your day is shot. You will have to plan and execute your morning and afternoon in a way to ensure you don't miss that bus. If, on the other hand, there are buses throughout the day, say, every ten minutes, then you can be more casual. If you miss the first bus, no big deal, you'll catch the next one. Breaking work down into smaller pieces works much the same way. In fact, it helps us in multiple ways; let's look first at reducing the number of dependencies.

From a development perspective, packing a lot of work into releases means many more dependencies will have to be managed across initiatives and impacted applications. From a testing perspective, downstream environments (such as system test <ST> and user acceptance test <UAT>) have to manage much more information in terms of application versions and especially test data, which complicate and slow down the process. The complexity of the test-data increase is proportional to the number of pair-wise relationships that exist within the datasets required for testing. As such, the testing complexity will increase non-linearly (perhaps proportional to the square of the dependent systems) and from a release and change perspective; there is a lot of coordination necessary given how much is being changed at one time.

All this work to manage all of the dependencies found in medium to large enterprises eliminates any potential savings one might get from batching work into a single delivery. In addition, the possibility of having to pull some work out of a release (due to quality or business readiness or some other reason) sometimes leads to complicated source-code management (feature branches in some cases), which further complicates the process of merging frequently into the trunk. These types of practices also serve to drive up technical debt. So, when we look at the problem from this angle, we understand why the results we are seeing make perfect sense.

> *Productivity is inversely proportional to the*
> *number of dependencies in a release.*

IT

Automation needs to take on a whole new meaning, and the way we look at automation needs to change dramatically—and quickly! Just as Charlie's father in *Charlie and the Chocolate Factory*[81] had to change from being the guy who put the caps on to the guy who maintained the capping machine, many of the roles in IT will need to change dramatically. Robotic process automation and self-service API access are the tip of the iceberg. Micro-services will need to be built and maintained. Codeless solutions will soon be mainstream, and the cloud will replace many one-off hardware builds. As this happens, we'll need to build the tools that will enable the identification and flow of work.

The ability to visualize the work and see the artifact flow is the key to knowing where bottlenecks exist and where work is building up. There is more about this in the "Value Stream Architecture" and "Theory of Constraints" sections of this book.

Process visibility. Complex input management and team notification of availability is a subject of authors and several software vendors. We are working to address this using the Deterministic Process Design® model and software tools that will facilitate the flow of the work and the collection of metrics about the flow, and it will make the work visible to the organization. Look for more information on this on our website (StandingOnShoulders.us) and the Deterministic Process Design® website (DeterministicProcessDesign.com).

---

[81] https://en.wikipedia.org/wiki/Charlie_and_the_Chocolate_Factory_(film)

III. HOW

Change Execution

Crawl, walk, run.

Applying Dickens to Deming

> *It was the best of times, it was the worst of times, it was the age of wisdom, it was the age of foolishness, it was the epoch of belief, it was the epoch of incredulity, it was the season of Light, it was the season of Darkness, it was the spring of hope, it was the winter of despair, we had everything before us, we had nothing before us.*
> —Charles Dickens, *A Tale of Two Cities*

At times, you may use the phrases above to describe the spectrum of feelings present during your digital transformation journey. Incredible things will be performed by some of your leading, innovative teams, things like reducing the time to run a test suite from hours to minutes or going from deploying once every two to three months to deploying two to three times a week or reducing the lead time of a story from creation to deployment from eighty days to under a week.

But at the same time, challenges will remain, such as over-governance of change control requiring more manual reports and endless CAB (change approval board) meetings. Or having request processes for simple infrastructure changes that could take weeks to be accomplished. Or the inability of a team to make and promote their own database changes, having instead to submit them to a central team of DBAs, who have way too much work in progress to respond quickly to the new requests.

Carmen: John Willis (noted DevOps author) gives a talk called "From Deming to DevOps" about how Deming's thinking is at the core of the DevOps philosophy particularly regarding Systems Thinking. For those not familiar with Deming, we encourage you to research his history and also the famous "Red Bead Experiments." Many of the non-value-added work done in large enterprises can be categorized by as an example of a red bead experiment (e.g., multiple levels of estimation). Deming's *Out of the Crisis* remains the classic read on lean and continuous improvement principles.

I was introduced to Deming's concepts at Bell Labs in the eighties. It is not surprising that Deming would be present in the culture of Bell Labs, given that his cohort, Walter A. Shewhart, worked there from its foundation in 1925 until his retirement in 1956. At Bell Labs, the concepts of PDCA (plan/do/check/act) and continuous improvement were so embedded into the culture, I would say it was the air we breathed.

While Deming certainly paved the way for the practices that are now part of Agile, Lean, and DevOps, perhaps Dickens in 1859 also provided a glimpse into how selfless leadership (like those exhibited by one of the heroes of his story – Sydney Carton) would be needed to transform our industry. While we are not suggesting that the prospect of facing the guillotine is necessary to attempt to transform a large organization, make no mistake that along with the accomplishment of lots of great things, there will be more than a few bumps in the road.

There is a lot of evidence to support that taking action drives changes in thinking. It's also important to identify what behaviors we want to change along with how and why we want to change them. An interesting article on making cultural changes suggests that we can do this in an evolutionary way or a disruptive way.[82] Further, that we will be most

---

[82] https://www.forbes.com/sites/erikaandersen/2012/08/17/3-things-you-can-do-to-change-peoples-behavior/#4052378e7a0a

likely to be successful if we make the new behaviors easy, rewarding, and normal. We can shift where we are on the evolutionary-disruptive scale, maybe, by bundling changes in a way that makes sense contextually. For example, if we reorganize our development organization *and* change the tools they use to execute, along with corresponding shift in the cultural environment (e.g., personnel policies that ease dress codes, support job sharing or flexible hours, or add amenities like free coffee), and we do this in an orchestrated fashion, we can instantiate a paradigm shift that is authentic and coordinates and supports the new "talk and walk."

Start Small

As with other improvement initiatives, it pays to start small and build momentum. Changing the culture of a large organization is not something that can be forced, even if there is top-down support. However, many times, the types of initiatives that don't have full support to begin with can be expanded, as described in the 2017 Forum reference "Expanding Pockets of Greatness."[83]

By finding one area that is open to working in the product model, you can demonstrate that it is *possible to be done*. That changes the conversation from "This can't be done here" to "This is how it can be done here."

A great example of this is the talk by Cindy Payne and Jim Grafmeyer[84] about the Nationwide DevOps experiments.

Label This as an Experiment

In order to run an experiment, there needs to be criteria to determine if, in fact, it is successful. Examples of metrics to track include flow metrics (e.g., flow of business value stories). One aspect of this relates to Deming's concept of quality circles. The team itself understands best what is inhibiting their flow and how to improve it. The team should use retrospectives to ask themselves why certain stories had shorter lead times than others and what improvements could be made. If there is a need for a change

---

[83] https://itrevolution.com/book/expanding-pockets-greatness/
[84] https://www.youtube.com/watch?v=9WAiFAgkO5g

that extends beyond this team, it can be escalated up to their leadership to apply Deming's concept of "systems thinking."[85]

Make the Experimental and the Improvement Work Visible

There needs to be CI (continuous improvement) work associated with any experiment. Per the Dominica DeGrandis book *Making Work Visible*,[86] make this CI work visible. It will take team bandwidth to adapt this model, so be transparent about it. Track blockers just as the team would for any other business deliverable and escalate blockers to their leaders to address.

Have Show-and-Tells and Invite Executives

One powerful way to move culture is to have retrospectives and then show-and-tells (at least once a month) that focus on the adoption of this model. Having CIOs share in the energy and excitement that the team has and also the successes and areas where they need help can be a powerful way to impact the executive mindset, which is necessary to expand the product model to other areas. CIOs feeling a sense of ownership in supporting the team in making this work will pave the way to future success.

Celebrate Small Wins

Many organizations are not good at celebrating and publicizing wins. We talk a lot about what is going wrong but not as much as what is working well. *Stories are powerful!* People remember stories that are told by the teams doing the work. When other teams see their peers having success, this is a powerful motivator, as it shows this is not just a theory but is possible right here, right now. Having the business leader talk about how this model is helping them succeed in the marketplace is extremely effective. Having teams tell their stories and sharing credit for success is a necessary component to building the critical mass to broader adoption.

---

[85] https://www.linkedin.com/pulse/systems-thinking-carmen-deardo/
[86] https://itrevolution.com/book/making-work-visible/

Have the Patience to Persevere

The journey ahead will seem daunting. It is necessary to reflect on how far you've come and not just how far there is to go. Reach out beyond your company to the broader DevOps community, to others who are on the same journey or who have already successfully demonstrated success in the product model. Have patience, persevere, keep the faith, and don't be afraid to ask for help. It won't be easy, but it will be satisfying to see the progress you will make.

> Jack: Involve practitioners in a sustained, meaningful, and transparent way. We were able to take our "tried and true" RUP-based processes and transform most of them into v1.0 of our Lean and Agile technology solution delivery processes. We built awareness and excitement for about three weeks with the announcement of a "Hackathon and Innovation Workshop." In addition to flyers and posters in building, e-mail, Yammer posts, and word of mouth, we also put up a website where individuals and teams could sign up and could "claim" the part of the process that was most important to them. The teams were self-forming, and we gave prizes for the best team banner/flag and best costumes, and we brought in tons of food and drinks. We had strategic resources that ensured teams in remote locations were connected through video conferencing (and sent them stickers and arts-and-crafts supplies, had food delivered, etc.), and we helped get the teams in their four locations connected to other teams. We had "kibitzers" who "poked their nose in everyone's business" to help drive collaborations and consistency across teams. We had senior leaders come to hand out "kind" bars, and we took a collective minute to commit to doing "a random act of kindness" within the next twenty-four hours. We had CIOs and VPs speak and be visibly present throughout the day to show executive support. It was a smashing success!

In the appendix is an updated process based on what we used then, although we have continued to polish it (that was actually the inaugural run). People had fun, and we maintained full fidelity and transparency of everything they did and the results of the day. To this day, you can trace the current practices (that were around then) back to the original team and what they came up with. It was a long, fun, and deeply engaging day for the 237 associates who gave up a Friday and made a real, meaningful, and lasting impact on what they do.

Let's now look at three different execution approaches. For ease of reference, we'll refer to them as *small*, *medium*, and *large*.

Small

This approach is focused on organizations with the smallest amount of necessary investment in technology. This might be because you have a small organization, or you are a small group within an organization, perhaps as a "pilot" group. Technology will be geared toward a centralized team perspective (meaning it is not spread across multiple locations) and tend toward simple tools and physical representations. This may be suitable, for example, for organizations that are technology averse for some reason (e.g., culture or general preference).

In some cases, it makes sense to use certain tools regardless of the size or relative sophistication of your organization. For example, Git[87] and GitHub[88] are sensible tools for source-code management and other processes whether you have two developers or two thousand. The software is free to use and has enterprise-level capabilities. For this approach, 3"x5" cards on a board (or even pinned on a corkboard or cube wall) may be enough. Consider the group, your culture, your budget, and your level of commitment to making this change. You will send clear messages, intended and otherwise, with these choices.

---

[87] https://git-scm.com
[88] https://github.com

The core practices of DevOps are source-code control, continuous integration, and automated testing leading to continuous delivery. These practices are well documented in several references, including *The DevOps Handbook*.[89] Organizations must begin here to implement practices and tools to provide these capabilities. As noted above, a tool based on Git (e.g., GitLab or GitHub), Jenkins,[90] or Circle CI[91] for continuous integration, as well as automation using Ruby[92] or Cucumber,[93] are some of the standards used for these practices. Moreover, as Dominica DeGrandis writes about in her book *Making Work Visible*,[94] it is necessary to make all your work visible (including dependencies and unplanned work) in a visual system or on a board that the team uses to track the progress of work. While there are tools like Jira[95] and LeanKit[96] (among others) for this, this can also be done simply using GitHub issues if the majority of the work is done by a small team with little or no dependencies.

No matter what size organization you are, you need to be focused on code quality and security. An open-source tool like SonarQube[97] can be integrated into your pipeline to ensure that the build is considered broken if any configured code quality rules are breached when code is checked in. Likewise, security tools like Fortify[98] and AppScan[99] can be integrated into your pipeline, along with some readily available open-source tools [100] that are free (or nearly free).

One open-source tool every organization should consider implementing is the Capital One"s Hygieia tool.[101] The brainchild of Topo Pal,

---

[89] https://itrevolution.com/book/the-devops-handbook/
[90] https://jenkins.io/
[91] https://circleci.com
[92] https://www.ruby-lang.org/en/
[93] https://cucumber.io
[94] https://itrevolution.com/book/making-work-visible/
[95] https://www.atlassian.com/software/jira
[96] https://leankit.com
[97] https://www.sonarqube.org
[98] https://software.microfocus.com/en-us/products/application-security-testing/overview
[99] https://www.ibm.com/security/application-security/appscan
[100] https://learn.techbeacon.com/units/47-powerful-open-source-app-sec-tools-you-should-consider
[101] http://capitalone.github.io/Hygieia/getting_started.html

this open-source dashboard provides visibility to the status of work, builds, deployments, and many other DevOps metrics used to monitor team activity and progress.

For small enterprises, pipeline and deployment capability is provided in the CI tools (Jenkins, Circle CI), which can be used for deployment. Of course, once the code is deployed, the "Ops" part of DevOps takes place in terms of monitoring the software in production. This is where tools like Splunk and New Relic are used to create alerts for and log events that require a response.

Base your decisions on your relative risk tolerance and your cost/benefit analysis, capabilities, and training—for example, Office 365˚ versus Google Docs.

Medium

The following approach will suit medium-sized companies, where a single visual management board, for example, cannot be seen by everyone. It is also suitable for organizations that have a bias toward technology (e.g., IT consulting firm). This approach will generally utilize more technology than the "small" approach. We'll focus on scalable tools that can grow with the organization and provided distributed team access. To the maximum extent possible, we'll identify open-source and web tools that don't require infrastructure and large IT investment.

An example of tools here might include something like WorkFusion RPA Express.[102] The basic tool is essentially free (although we know that "there's no such thing as a free lunch," sometimes referred to as TNSTAAFL), and you can begin to automate many of the things that eat away at your time. Of course, there are many other tools in this space from vendors (not free), including IBM's Automation Anywhere,[103] UiPath,[104] and Blue Prism˚.[105]

---

[102] https://www.workfusion.com/
[103] https://www.automationanywhere.com
[104] https://www.uipath.com
[105] https://www.blueprism.com/

In this situation, consider the need for a PPM (project and portfolio management) system to manage the portfolio of work being done. Once you get into larger organizations, there are obviously financial processes that must be managed, and there can be multiple portfolios of work.

The key here is to be able to visualize and trace work from a customer idea, which is to be funded, to the portfolio of work, where it can be prioritized, funded, and broken into features and stories. These can then be fed downstream into the backlog of your Agile teams to implement and deploy.

For medium enterprises, it may not be necessary to implement the larger-scale PPM systems, like Planview [106] and Clarity/Computer Associates PPM;[107] instead, select from the growing variety of leaner tools that are moving out of the Agile management space, like VersionOne[108] and TargetProcess.[109]

Even if you aren't implementing a version of Scaled Agile,[110] you will typically need to track work that crosses your development teams. For example, an idea that becomes a funded initiative will consist of a set of features, each of which will have multiple stories. The stories for a given feature may be directed to multiple teams.

Let's consider an idea that requires a front-end change (e.g., mobile/web page "system of engagement") and a back-end change to an administrative "system of record." In this case, you might have separate teams working on the front-end and back-end systems using a service-based API to pass information back and forth. You will need the ability to track this feature work visibly across teams and display the dependency.

In this case, PPM artifacts (e.g., idea -> initiative -> feature -> stories) need to have visibility and traceability across your delivery-value stream. An integration technology like Tasktop[111] is essential to flow artifacts automatically.

---

[106] https://www.planview.com/
[107] https://www.ca.com/us/products/ca-project-portfolio-management.html
[108] https://www.versionone.com/
[109] https://www.targetprocess.com/
[110] https://en.wikipedia.org/wiki/Scaled_agile_framework
[111] https://www.tasktop.com

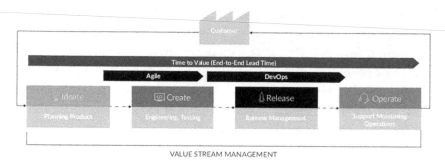

VALUE STREAM MANAGEMENT

Image 15. Value Stream Management.

Again, practices of configuration management (which should include more than just source code but should also include test-code and configuration information and database scripts) and continuous integration are essential, as is automated testing.

Medium-sized organizations should also consider using release-and-deployment tooling provided by XebiaLabs,[112] Electric Cloud,[113] and UrbanCode[114] (IBM/HCL) to provide the management, certification, and deployment of application releases into test and production environments.

Systems like Splunk[115] and New Relic[116] are more essential for larger enterprises. These are used not only for production, but monitoring should begin in test environments to amplify feedback loops (Gene Kim's "Second Way").

Large

This section applies to bigger organizations, especially those that have multiple locations and require scalability. Here we'll address open-source and commercially available enterprise-level tools that can support large organizations and the most sophisticated capabilities currently available.

---

[112] https://www.xebialabs.com
[113] https://electric-cloud.com/
[114] https://developer.ibm.com/urbancode/products/
[115] https://www.splunk.com
[116] https://newrelic.com

The biggest difference for large enterprises is on the left-hand side of the value stream, starting from the business hypothesis of an idea and flowing this into work for your Agile teams to design, implement, and deploy. Large enterprises are more likely to have regulatory issues and financial considerations that will require using a full-capability PPM tool, like Planview.

A good list of tools that can be integrated into your value stream is available from Tasktop,[117] on their website. Another great reference is the XebiaLabs' "Periodic Table of DevOps Tools."[118]

So, How Do We Get Started?

We start with the value-stream maps, which we explained at the beginning of this book.

Step 1: Identify and put all your planned business projects on your VSM

This is the work that is focused on what your organization produces. It might actually be creating your product. It could be an improvement to your production process tooling or the tools (or systems) that your company uses to produce the value that you sell or provide.

Step 2: Identify and put all your planned internal projects on your VSM

These are the projects that you do to support any internal processes or work. It could be your enterprise resource planning system (like SAP® or Oracle®/PeopleSoft), the system that calculates and manages author royalties, or the systems that supports customer service and billing.

Step 3: Identify and put all your operational work on your VSM

This is the work that you have to do to keep your own processes operating, such as sharpening tool edges, grooming a backlog, resolving technical

---

[117] https://www.tasktop.com/integrations
[118] https://xebialabs.com/periodic-table-of-devops-tools/

debt, and conducting proactive counseling or performance-management sessions with associates.

Step 4: Identify and put all your current unplanned work on your VSM

This is a big black hole of time consumption that you'd really like to avoid, such as defect remediation, down (non-functioning) equipment, and issues resolution related to the environment or people.

Do you have a lot of aggregation in specific areas?

There are many reasons why work will aggregate in some areas. We need to understand why. Sometimes it can be a good thing, but this is not often the case.

Getting WIP under Control

Taking a step back, what are your golf balls? Golf balls?

> Jack: At the beginning of 2018, I took my team to an off-site location, so we could discuss and plan our approach for our work and our team dynamics for the year. We watched a video together, and we invite you to do the same. There are many versions of this. Just search for "The Jar of Life," or try this link: https://youtu.be/m0hqBIugr7I.

We can apply this concept of prioritization and constraints at multiple levels. We must stratify our work, so we can focus on the right things. Making all the work we do visible and acknowledging it is the first step.

Architecting Our Future State

As we get down to the nuts and bolts of planning our future state, there are a couple of things that we need to add that were probably not on our landscape before. "Future you" will want to kick "current you" if you don't layer them in now.

Architecture is our first actual step on this journey. Up until now, it's been preparation and consideration. Our architecture needs to address several core needs:

- Speed
- Resilience
- Future-proofing

Architecting for Speed

While we talk about using APIs and micro-services as part of a digitally-enabled architecture, we usually refer to these as good general practices for cloud enablement. What we don't talk about is how to use these concepts to architect for speed of business capability delivery.

If a system is providing services for other systems to access that require speed of delivery (e.g., a system of engagement (SoE) that is being frequently changed to experiment with different ways of selling a product), then providing an API/micro-service for that SoE to access allows changes to occur more quickly. This implies that you are refactoring a monolithic architecture, you should work with the product manager to prioritize the creation of APIs/micro-services where their usage will enable speed of delivery for the consuming (SoE) systems.

Systems Thinking—Designing for Resiliency

> Carmen: I was very fortunate to spend the first twenty-five years of my career at Bell Labs working in the network systems area. I worked on the architecture and design of the core systems used in the AT&T Network. This included systems that did all the front-end or intelligent network processing of calls (e.g., 800 service), which, in its peak, was a multi-billion-dollar revenue stream.

These systems were designed to run in a "dark office," which meant there were no onsite personnel to support them. As with all telecommunications systems involved with handling calls, the performance and availability of these systems were very high. The availability was "four nines" or "five nines," which meant these systems were designed to be 99.99 or 99.999 percent available.

Level of Availability	Percent of Uptime	Downtime per Year	Downtime per Day
1 Nine	90%	36.5 days	2.4 hrs.
2 Nines	99%	3.65 days	14 min.
3 Nines	99.9%	8.76 hrs.	86 sec.
4 Nines	99.99%	52.6 min.	8.6 sec.
5 Nines	99.999%	5.25 min.	.86 sec.
6 Nines	99.9999%	31.5 sec.	8.6 msec

Image 16. The Table of Nines.

As you can see from the Table of Nines, a system that is "four nines" has a downtime less than an hour a year, and a "five-nines" system is down less than a five and a half minutes a year! Contrast that with most front-end systems today, which typically have availability in the area of two nines to three nines.

Also, note that availability, in this case, includes both planned and unplanned downtime. Often, non-functional requirements are written only to cover a system's unplanned downtime. However if a system is down, do you as a user really care if it was "planned" or "unplanned"? Especially in a global world that is becoming 24/7 in terms of user's expectations, the idea that it's okay to shut a system down over a weekend or in the middle of the night in North America is not going to fly.

> Carmen: The hardest work on a project was the generic update where it was necessary to keep the system operating while it was being upgraded. Think of this as a patient having to continue to do their job while undergoing an operation. This required having redundant systems and hardware and very sophisticated software engineering approaches.
>
> One example was the upgrade of a system that was used for storing and accessing cellular voice messages. Each user was assigned a mailbox, which resided on a

server. If it was necessary to upgrade that server, it was determined that it might be okay for a small period of time for a user not to be able to retrieve messages but that the ability to leave messages for this user should always be maintained. This required that an algorithm be implemented where other mailbox servers could take messages for a user whose host mailbox was being upgraded and then sending them when that host mailbox server was restored. While that doesn't sound that complicated, one needs to consider that you don't want to flood a mailbox server after it has just come back into service following an upgrade. So, a lot of work had to go into engineering an algorithm that could ensure the messages were restored in the shortest period while still not putting that server into overload.

Another complicating factor was that the system needed to operate when some of the servers were on version X and others were on version X+1. Therefore, this type of compatibility had to be designed into the overall design of the systems.

Another factor to consider was that these high-performance, high-availability systems were implemented without the kind of clustering and cloud capabilities that are available today. So, to implement a network with active/active components, it was necessary to do that "by hand," that is, using highly-available systems from vendors like DEC[119] (Digital Equipment Corporation) or Stratus Computer[120] and building custom hardware to accomplish this. The key to these systems' software availability was the processing control subsystem. This subsystem was designed to initialize the system, keep it running, and recover quickly from any errors. This was so important to us that we created technology and

---

[119] https://en.wikipedia.org/wiki/Digital_Equipment_Corporation
[120] https://www.stratus.com/

patented it.[121] It is just one example of the type of design that went into providing this type of capability.

Now we don't imagine that you're going to need to develop technology to maintain or synchronize your systems. But, you do need to think about what today's expectations are around availability of your systems to internal and external customers. And let's face it, your availability issues may have nothing to do with your systems, upgrades, patches, etc., there are also plenty of other bad actors out there …

Relationship to DevOps, SRE, and the Chaos Monkey

While this may (or may not) sound fascinating, one might ask, "What does this have to do with modern DevOps practices?" Well, to implement these kinds of systems, a number of techniques utilized today as DevOps practices were used to guarantee high performance and high availability.

The first is the concept of SRE. Site reliability engineering[122] is a system that Google implemented to address three types of work:

1. Minimize MTTR (mean time to recovery)
2. Improve system availability where SysA = (1 - MTTR/MTBF)
3. Improve service availability where SrvA = multipliers of SysA in service dependency chain

(MTBF: mean time between failures)

MTTR and MTBF are key components of system availability. As we increase the number of systems required to accomplish a transaction or process, a modest change has a significant effect on the whole (e.g., three systems with 97 percent availability versus those same systems with 99 percent availability).

---

[121] http://patft.uspto.gov/netacgi/nph-Parser?Sect1=PTO2_and_Sect2=HITOFF_and_p=1_and_u=/netahtml/PTO/search-bool.html_and_r=2_and_f=G_and_l=50_and_col=AND_and_d=PTXT_and_s1=DeArdo.INNM._and_s2=Carmen.INNM._and_OS=IN/DeArdo+AND+IN/Carmen_and_RS=IN/DeArdo+AND+IN/Carmen

[122] https://landing.google.com/sre/

.97 *.97 *.97 = 91 percent available

If we increase availability of all three systems, then

.99 *.99 *.99 = 97 percent available

As we consider what this means from the perspective of how we measure availability, our availability rating would only reach the first "tier," or 1-nine.

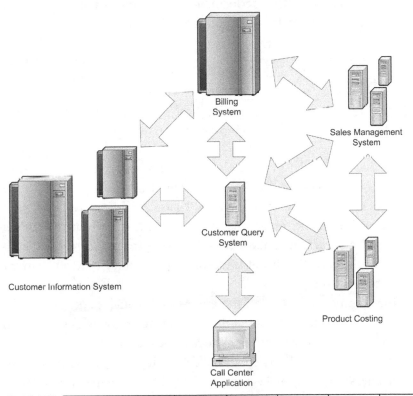

	Call Center	Query	CIS	Billing	Sales	Product	TOTAL
Scenario A	97%	99%	95%	99%	97%	98%	86%
Scenario B	98%	99%	98%	99%	98%	98%	90%
Scenario C	99%	99%	99%	99%	99%	99%	94%

Image 17. Systems availability example.

Depending on the number of subsystems within this architecture and their performance, we could see dramatic impact on availability. In this use case, we look at the application that a call center operator might use to handle a request for a new product for an existing customer, in which case the query system would have to get the customer information from a system and then, using that information, get any billing system impacts (such as the packaging costs for this type of product) along with any contracts in place in the sales-management system and new product-cost estimates from the product-costing system. If we look at how these systems together perform, here are several scenarios that may more closely approximate our expectations today:

	Call Center	Query	CIS	Billing	Sales	Product	TOTAL
Scenario A	97%	99%	95%	99%	97%	98%	86%
Scenario B	98%	99%	98%	99%	98%	98%	90%
Scenario C	99%	99%	99%	99%	99%	99%	94%

Image 18. Three nines to four nines to five nines.

Of course, in today's complex technological environment, the number of systems involved continues to grow dramatically. As we drive applications into micro-services and API-based architectures, we'll need to keep an eye on the impact that has versus the improvements we get from cloud abstraction of hardware leading to probably better availability. We could see a significant trade-off in performance with too many disparate functions.

The common factor in all these is MTTR, which is defined in the "State of DevOps Report" as the time it takes to restore service after an unplanned outage or service impairment. The reason that this is important is that it mitigates the risk associated with deploying more frequently. The business partners will be more comfortable with deploying software more frequently if they believe that if anything goes wrong in that deployment, it can be rectified very quickly, before there are any customer impacts to business.

Minimizing recovery time requires the following events to occur as quickly as possible:

1. Detection of a problem
2. Isolation of the problem to determine what is needed for recovery
3. Recovery from the problem

Following the event, we gain a better understanding of failure events, enabling us to reduce their probability of reoccurrence and improve MTBF (see John Allspaw discuss this on YouTube).[123] As such, the SRE role looks for opportunities to automate recovery actions from alerts or errors that are produced by the system. By doing this, it eliminates (or minimizes) the cases where human interaction is needed, which increases the potential for customers to be impacted.

An example of this type of thinking was present at Bell Labs, in areas such as automating the role of an operator who was onsite and accessing the console output of a system. Typically, the console output includes messages that require human intervention. This includes things like a notification that a process has died, a file system is full, a disk has too many bad block errors, etc. Because the telecom systems were in a dark-office setting, there was no operator present to read the console output in real time. In many cases, operators might have to drive thirty minutes to reach an office if there was indication of a problem that required some maintenance activity be performed onsite (e.g., reboot the system or enter a command to clean up a file system). As such, part of the design of the system was to automatically detect these problems and take actions, such as

1. Automatically detect a process death and restart the process or entire application
2. Clean up a file system
3. Remap a disk

So, while Bell Labs certainly didn't coin the term "SRE," this type of systems thinking was certainly used in the development and implementation of these systems to achieve the four and five nines that are expected by today's users and customers.

---

[123] https://www.youtube.com/watch?v=xA5U85LSk0M

Jack: This concept has also been around in other ways for quite some time. We had an IBM service technician show up unexpectedly once with a replacement DASD (hard drive) that was beginning to fail. One of our AS/400s had "phoned home" to report early warning signs of impending trouble. In a consulting gig with an insurance company a few years later, we built an operational plan for a new data center using MTBF (mean time between failures) data for predictive maintenance to avoid failures of critical systems. This saved time and avoided failures, which practically eliminated downtime and data loss. We mitigated the relatively low cost of the inexpensive components by moving them to test regions to mitigate. Then, if there were failures, that would facilitate "unplanned disaster recovery testing."

Chaos Monkey

Chaos Monkey[124] is a capability developed at Netflix circa 2011, which, in their words, does the following: "Chaos Monkey is responsible for randomly terminating instances in production to ensure that engineers implement their services to be resilient to instance failures." The concept of introducing random failures (both software and hardware) was also part of the standard work that was performed at Bell Labs to "harden" systems. As such, Bell would do something called "operational testing" for each release.

Typical test conditions:

1. Introduce twice the engineered capacity of transactions loads (generally, this meant call processing and update processing).
2. Introduce routine network or maintenance support technician activities.

---

[124] https://netflix.github.io/chaosmonkey/

3. Run a script that would randomly send termination signals (kill -9) to processes.
4. Randomly fail or take hardware out of service.
5. Analyze error and maintenance logs to ensure that the proper operations were being logged and alerts were being generated.

Test expectations:

1. The system would recover as designed when automatically possible without going into overload or losing any calls or updates to the customer database (e.g., updates to customers' 800 service records).
2. When there was a need for human intervention (e.g., replacing a failed piece of hardware), the appropriate maintenance alarms would be generated to quickly determine the problem and resolution.

This type of testing found many problems in how the system operated under load. In the case of at least one vendor, it found deadlock issues in how these events were being processed in the kernel. The apocalyptic test was to put the system under twice the load and then fail half the duplicated power, which would cause half of the all hardware to fail. The system was still expected to run under this load while processing all the maintenance events associated with a system, losing half its available hardware devices.

This type of testing produced systems that were highly available with quick MTTRs based on applying automation whenever possible. While they used to be unique to telecom, these types of practices are becoming mainstream due to Google and Netflix and their incorporation into DevOps practices.

The key concepts remain the same:

- Resiliency designed into systems
- Automate the detection, isolation and recovery actions when failures due occur.

The reality is that despite our best efforts at resiliency and fault tolerance, hardware and software will fail. So, plan and design for it to mitigate the impact on customers.

Denial of Service (DOS) Attacks

The concept of DOS wasn't applicable during the era of developing the systems to handle 800 traffic, but plenty of thinking was applied to the concept of network management where systems could be overloaded due to broad or localized events.

These algorithms were designed to shed traffic in the case where too much traffic was being received, so that it could not be processed before the switch sending it would time out. They were also designed to send back "call or code" gapping signals to the switch, which would then throttle traffic as close to the source as possible.

These algorithms proved their worth when some situations occurred that could hardly be planned for. One such situation was the infamous "Captain Crunch" scenario, named for the eponymous breakfast cereal.

> Carmen: Captain Crunch became an 800 customer mostly for any calls dealing with quality assurance issues, as customers called to comment on their cereal. As such, the expected load generated for them was expected to be very low. Unlike an airline or hotel chain, for example, the toll-free number was not used to make reservations and generate sales. It was simply to provide a support number for customers to use.
>
> We were very surprised when, one morning, a system that was handling the calls for Captain Crunch went into overload. While the system continued to function properly and handle calls, we still needed to investigate why this was happening. We were surprised to find that the calls to the Captain Crunch number were over ten times what we expected. This peak quickly passed shortly after the breakfast hours in the US.

We discovered that new cereal boxes with a treasure map had recently been sold in grocery stores. Included with the map was an 800 number for clues or information to help find the treasure. Little did the company realize that children, eating their breakfast before going to school, would look at the map on the back of the box and start calling this number! They quickly had to update their customer record to play an automated response and then "strangle" (phase) out this type of cereal box. But by then, the legend of Captain Crunch was ingrained in the mindset of all of us who had experienced it.

So, the lesson here is to expect the unexpected. Design your systems to be resilient, and do not rely simply on the infrastructure provided (cloud or on-premise) without implementing additional ways for systems to react to unintended failures or overload situations. The only way to get good at this is to practice these in live (or near-live) environments.

Automation—We Have To! Here's Why and How We Can Get Started

In general, automation should be provided for repeatable activities in your value stream. These include things like continuous integration, code-quality analysis, test automation (including performance and security), release certification, deployment, monitoring, and feedback (both operational feedback on system performance and customer feedback on how features are being used, with links to business financials).

However, when starting this, one must prioritize and determine where the biggest return can be gained. One also needs to design automation using the same development processes one uses with code. For example, automated tests should be considered part of the product. This means that they should be designed for reuse, be code reviewed, and fall under source code control. Otherwise, you can end up with technical debt around automation tests and scripts that fall into disrepair. Tests may not kept up to date and start to fail regularly. The failures are then ignored, since they happen so frequently. This leads to loss of confidence in automation.

So, yes, automation is a necessary component if you wish to increase your delivery frequency and reduce lead times. However, care must be taken to apply software-engineering principles to automation tests and scripts.

For more detail on this, see Jez Humble's book *Continuous Delivery*.[125]

Advanced topics. Deterministic process design is defined as activity development and modeling, and associated process documentation, that enables automated provisioning, management, monitoring, and metrics reporting of activity accomplishment for specific results and outcomes. DPD is an advanced approach to modeling, designing, and documenting business processes that enables the automation of the full value stream, from ideation through technology deployment. As mentioned earlier, this has been done at a low level of automation but without truly visible or directly accessible systems. While the current work is not immediately available due to ongoing development and non-disclosure agreements, you can follow this development on our website and the Deterministic Process Design website (https://www.DeterministicProcessDesign.com).

---

[125] https://www.amazon.com/Continuous-Delivery-Deployment-Automation-Addison-Wesley/dp/0321601912

APPENDIX

A. Value-Stream Mapping

Value-stream mapping is a lean-management method for analyzing the current state and designing a future state for the series of events that take a product or service from its beginning through to the customer. A value stream focuses on areas of a firm that add value to a product or service, whereas a value chain refers to all of the activities within a company.[126]

Value-stream mapping (VSM) is among the most important exercises to understand what we do and where we can best improve what we do.

At first it seems deceptively easy. After all, any senior leader knows what we do and how the "whole thing" works, right? Actually, no. Not often does any one person have a true view of what is done across the full value stream. In fact, when we get right down to it, there is likely not even a full vision of the value stream, let alone detailed knowledge of each step along that trail, from someone's idea to the delivery of the manifestation, value, or result of the full chain. It starts and ends with the customer.

In their book *Value Stream Mapping*, Karen Martin and Mike Osterling[127] list five reasons for doing VSM:

1. Effectively establishes strategic direction for improvement
2. Provides highly visible full cycle view from start to finish
3. Deepens organizational understanding of value delivery for better decision making and work design
4. Quantitative nature enables data-driven strategy decisions
5. Reflects flow of work and value from the *customer's view* versus internally focused process maps

---

[126] "Value Stream Mapping," *Wikipedia*, last modified July 3, 2018, https://en.wikipedia.org/wiki/Value_stream_mapping.

[127] https://www.ksmartin.com/books/value-stream-mapping/

They go on to list some additional benefits, including one that's a big issue in this book, which we've mentioned several times: it provides a visualization of frequently otherwise non-visible work. A value-stream map is also the starting point for systems thinking, and it can help us understand the impact of local optimization on other parts (such as the robot or Carmen's applesauce). I like Karen and Mike's idea of looking at the value-stream map as a blueprint of your business. This could be a great way to introduce new associates to the big picture of your organization in your new-hire orientation process.

It's hard to say which has more value, the act of doing the value stream mapping or the results. There is a ton of value in both! Making this a highly visible process and sharing the results has a lot of benefit to your organization, ranging from a tangible manifestation of commitment to improvement and acknowledging (and pursuing) opportunities for improvement. As people identify their parts and roles, they are better engaged, as seen through Gallup's question number eight: connection to the organizational mission and purpose. Seeing where they add value also enables everyone to connect with how customers (both internal and external) see and experience the organization and their contribution to it.

Although it is technically not part of this process, the value-stream map also ties into our process maps. (We'll do this later on, not now or even soon.) Implementing role- and process standard work is vital, particularly if we want drill down to the level of doing Deterministic Process Design®. The ability to then automate the process by integrating the entire chain from ideation through profitability reporting, with notifications and workflow, makes every part visible and data-driven.

When comes to doing the value-stream mapping, there are few things that you need to do first to prepare. First, find or select a facilitator. If you are in a large organization and have access to shared resources that include an experienced facilitator, that may be a good route.[128] Experience is also important, as there will be times when first instincts lead to suboptimal results. It is much better in the long run to have someone who's done it before.

---

[128] **NB**: Having someone who is impartial and not subject to political influences might be more important than you might think at first.

Planning

- Determine your approach/selection of facilitator.
- Get executive sponsorship.
- Determine the VSM team structure and size.
    - It's a tough balance between keeping it as small as possible and providing sufficient representation of your domains.
    - It needs to have the right mix of "juice," knowledge, and soft skills.
- Begin to understand, confirm, and map.
    - Scope and objectives
    - Sacred cows and boundaries
- Get commitments for time, location, and logistics.
- Collect current, historical, and projected data.
- Prepare organizational units for Gemba.[129]
- Prepare for "gotchas."
    - Staying out of the weeds
    - Time commitments and staying focused
- Discuss staying in house or taking a retreat approach
- Discuss and prepare
    - Intended outcomes
    - Personas (including potential competitors).
- Collect market intelligence, trends, and predictions.

Assemble the Team

Leadership buy-in is critical, and selection of team structure and size must be a part of that conversation. The executive sponsor *must* have the "juice" to make things happen, regardless of location in the organization and resources to execute.

---

[129] https://en.wikipedia.org/wiki/Gemba

The Value-Stream Map

There are three components to a value stream map:

1. Work flow
2. Information flow
3. Timeline

Metrics Are a Key Part, Not Optional

Data is essential. That's why we started collecting it early in our planning. The VSM is a snapshot in time, and it will not be reflective in all cases. That said, baseline it.

Start with What You Have

Do a Gemba walk with the whole team. Take a look at all the processes together. For the first time, it probably makes sense to start at the beginning. For most organizations, this is ideation, but depending on the organization, it could be engineering, sales, or marketing.

Do you have any process flows, maps, or documentation? We're aware of one organization that started off with an old set of document relationships that implied a flow and organizational structure of the incumbent methodology (based on RUP), which used their project documentation process as an initial work-flow analog. There are plenty of opportunities to correct, update, and refine as you go, so don't worry about being too perfect or too detailed now. Start with what you have, as close to the beginning of the process as you can (where the order is taken, where "pre-sales engineering gets a lead" or maybe when a lead comes in from an advertising campaign), and work your way through the process until the value is delivered to the customer.

Later, we'll take it the other direction; after the first pass, we will start at the end and work our way back upstream. This is helpful for several reasons, one of which is to help us look at the processes from a pull perspective (remember that?).

When designing your approach and detailing the plan, figure out how you're going to tackle your process and include the facilitator in the planning so that person can help avoid common pitfalls. Then make sure you communicate that plan, along with enough information regarding time ranges so teams can be ready (and so you don't show up while everyone is out to lunch or on a shift change).

Verb-noun nomenclature. It is helpful to identify the component of your value stream by naming it with an action verb (describing the action) and noun (describing the outcome or focus).

Focus on outcomes and results; intentions, not tools! Overreliance on tools is an easy trap, especially when we are tool-focused in our business, whether those tools are software tools or CNC machines. Don't fall for it.

Day One

Get the team together in a space where they can work without interruption or distraction and where they can keep materials, supplies, drafts, and access to company information stores and information. There are two schools of thought regarding whether sequestration should be on site or off site. How many sites you have, and their relative geographic dispersion is also an input.

Some think that on-site sequestration is good, as it provides direct and easy access to resources, teams, and facilities. Another approach is a "retreat" style of complete immersion, with scheduled Gemba walks. There are significant pros and cons to each. A lot of it may be determined by who needs to participate and what they can/will commit to doing.

Step 1: Gather the Team

The team should assemble in their temporary working space to become acquainted, discuss "rules of engagement" and review or create their charter. This is a good time to discuss:

- Objectives
  o Tangible
  o Intangible
  o Negotiable
  o Non-negotiable

- Expectations
  - Outcomes
  - Behaviors
    - "Ranks" come off, no titles or levels should be used, all are equal collaborators
    - Everyone on the team should give and expect humility and respect
    - Curiosity and true interest should be the primary approach, for understanding
    - There is no room for any intimidation and strive for proactively non-accusatory
    - A non-judgmental demeanor and tone is essential to getting honest feedback
- It is essential that the discussions and finding be completely fact-based, with no emotion or drama, and clear expectations are set up front about:
  - Scope and boundaries
  - Non-negotiable issues or processes
  - Readiness to hear unpleasant truths and unexpected realities
- It is important that the team "feels the pain" that associates bear routinely
- Understand the dysfunction

Step 2: Create the First Cut

Based on what is known (thought) by group, create a starting point.

- Use whatever is readily available. This is not a research project at this point.
- High level is fine. Avoid getting to anything that is done by an individual. Documenting the work at a group or team level is the goal.
  - Create Post-Its with
    - Name (action-verb)
    - Group
    - Where it comes from

- Where it goes to
- Who executes activity
  o Post them on the wall showing the flow from the beginning to the end.
    - Number each with a number (increment in tens, e.g., 10, 20, 30).
    - These are just for reference. Using tens enables easier insertion later without having to re-do labels.

Create data entry points/labels for each Post-It with:

- Process Time (how long does it take to do, a.k.a. effort)
- Lead Time (how long does it take to get through, a.k.a. Duration)
- percent Accurate and Complete

These will be our initial metrics. The key to this is how things are working, not how we wish things worked (or designed them to work).

Step 3: The First Gemba

The first Gemba has multiple objectives, including getting team together and giving them a shared experience within which to start to gel as a team. Keep the team together; do not let a "divide and conquer" mindset happen.

Walk through the stream as documented, from beginning to end. Prepare and coach to avoid assumptions. Avoiding coming across as accusatory or judgmental, and be genuinely curious and respectful. Remind what a gift unvarnished feedback is, and reward it generously with sincere thanks and graciousness. Take lots of notes. Ask many open-ended questions that get to root causes and core issues. Dig for understanding and don't overpromise. Listen, confirm, and summarize. Let them know you got it right.

Collect data and write it down! For the three data elements above, get the consensus from the practitioners for best, worst, and typical. This will help you get a feel for the range and variability.

Things to watch for or pay attention to:

- Service-level agreements (SLAs)
- Rework
- Batching
- Amount of work in process (WIP)
- Availability issues
  - People
  - Systems
  - Tools
  - Materials
  - Space
- Multitasking or context switching
- Prioritization practices and/or work-selection criteria
- Visual job aids, performance information, etc.
- Quality process/checks
  - Incoming/entrance criteria
  - Outgoing/exit criteria
- Scrap or rejects
- What is the "Five-S" situation?[130]

The Five Ss describe how the workplace is set up and how it is maintained.

1. *Seiri* (sort)
2. *Seiton* (straighten, set)
3. *Seiso* (shine, sweep)
4. *Seiketsu* (standardize)
5. *Shitsuke* (sustain)

Is it organized in a way that is conducive to the operations or work at hand? Are the tools and job aids readily available? Are the standards clear and the metrics, measurements, and progress posted visibly? Are the workers demonstrating attention to quality and care for themselves, each other, and the work environment? Collectively, these are key indicators about the team, their leaders, and the group culture and its operation within the rest of the organization.

---

[130] http://leansixsigmadefinition.com/glossary/5s/

Sustainability is the "S" that most teams (and leaders) find hardest to achieve. Entropy reigns unless there is a design for sustainability. Things will likely regress without a specific plan and follow-up. Especially when any kind of pressure is applied, we tend to go back to our "old, comfortable" ways.

Step 4: Bring It Back

Bring it all back "home" and talk about it while it is fresh.

- Do you need to add some Post-Its?
- Have you filled out the metrics data?
- Are you ready to do some diagramming?

Standard notation is good but not really important at this point. Your facilitator should help with tips about how to avoid "painting yourself into a corner." We might have multiple paths (either from the start or from what we found), in which case we'll need to identify the critical path (much like the Project Management Institute's PMBOK[131] version). That's what we'll use for our first analysis. Add a timeline along the bottom that captures the through-put, or total lead time/total duration for the process from start to finish. Now add the actual process time for all of them together, or total effort. What is the difference between the two? Usually it's quite a lot. Now take the total effort and divide it by the total lead time. The result is your action ratio. This is a relative flow indicator and your baseline for later comparison with the results of your improvements (i.e., it will let you compare "apples to apples").

Consider and review what you have with these questions in mind:

- Does it seem right? (Sometimes this is called the "sniff test.")
- How does it match up with what you expected?
- Does it correspond to standard performance reporting information (if available)?
- Did you uncover any surprises? What dysfunctions did you find?

Okay, that's a pretty full day one in most cases!

---

[131] https://search.pmi.org/default.aspx?q=critical+path

Depending on how you've decided to approach this, after either a good night's sleep in their own bed or at breakfast in a retreat format, the team will likely start off by talking about the prior day. That is good! Capture the thoughts and ideas that have accumulated overnight, but try not to dig into them or try to solve them yet. Next, walk through previous day's results on the diagram. Look for the flow and where it is disrupted or impeded. Consider this process from a "machine" perspective, how the overall "system" works. Look for where there are (or could/should be) feedback loops. If you have a trained facilitator, you might come back the next morning to a "pretty" value stream map. For the team, using a hands-on, manual approach is best to really get engaged and into the details. However, there are many good tools available to help with much of the distribution and readability (not to mention portability, if you're doing this off-site). Here's what a Value Stream Map (VSM) looks like in general:

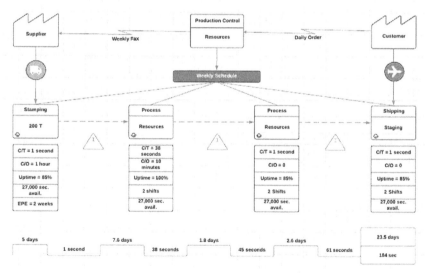

Created in Lucidchart (www.lucidchart.com)[132]
Image 19. Value-stream map example.

---

[132] Learn more about this tool and VSM at https://www.lucidchart.com/pages/value-stream-mapping, and use this tool to create your own VSM at https://www.lucidchart.com/pages/examples/value-stream-mapping.

You will notice there are some differences in how they have chosen to collect and represent their data. This is to be expected, and while we have some ideas about general data and analysis, you will find the right data to collect and metrics to monitor that will suit the needs of your leadership and stakeholders. On day two, we should also go back to the Gemba. This time, however, we don't start at the beginning of the process; we start at the end and work our way "upstream." Working our way upstream gives the team an opportunity to revisit with a different perspective. We also want to look at how we could consider thinking and acting in a "pull" mechanism versus the traditional "push"[133] approach that most organizations have used. The advantages are multiple, but in this context, we're looking for the opportunity for teams to be most efficient by managing their own Work In Progress (WIP) and pulling work in only when they have the capacity to undertake that work, as discussed in great detail earlier in this book.

In this "second cut," we should pay attention to Key Performance Indicators (KPIs), goals, and results, particularly as they are present visibly. What is being used in terms of visual management systems? We should see evidence on display regarding things like cycle times, defects, lost-time injuries, units completed, and other ways of keeping track and communicating accomplishments, concerns, and performance indicators. This second pass also provides the opportunity to confirm conclusions reached the first time through. It gives the team to "deconflict" differences of understanding between process steps and what different team members heard before and clarify any confusion. Then the team should head back to "home base" to make any updates necessary to the VSM before committing it as the "baseline."

The "Day After"

As we look at the steps and processes on our diagram, we see room for improvement. To some degree, we should begin to consider that now as a way of defining the scope for our improvements. Within the context of this book, this helps us reach our goal of documenting the current state

---

[133] https://en.wikipedia.org/wiki/Push%E2%80%93pull_strategy

value-stream map. As a standalone exercise, it would be silly to stop here without making improvements. But in this context, we use the rest of the book to consider the changes we should make that may go beyond the "normal" value-stream mapping approach for an organization. However, let's consider how we might choose to identify that scope.

Essentialism

Essentialism is a powerful tool to use when considering what we should do and not do as individuals and organizations. The removal of non-essential work and tasks provides many benefits. Among the most important to us is the reduction in WIP, the focus of resources on the highest value work, the acceleration of remaining work through lower utilization rates, and the increase in capacity for temporary (or even permanent) increases in demand or growth. Increased velocity of throughput, especially with improved quality, reduces our costs and increases the value created for and received by our customers.

Lean (and Associate Perceptions and Fears)

A not-funny gallows-humor joke at some companies is that lean stands for "Less Employees Are Needed." This is very much a culture play. Before beginning any effort like this, there should be a clear decision and a direction should be set regarding expected outcomes. In some organizations, there is a culture and leadership commitment to a predominantly associate workforce. So, when reductions in headcount necessarily become part of the appropriate result, they take place in the ranks of contractors first, not employees, to the maximum extent possible. However, people fear the unknown and typically expect the worst, no matter what. You really cannot overstate the importance of continuing to "show the love" and prove that you truly value them and will not make their worst fears come true. That said, if that is the reality, you owe it to those whose lives will be disrupted to be quick, humane, and compassionate. The increased capacity of associates that is realized can and should be focused on higher value work, improved products that drive growth, and reduced cost due to faster throughput, which reduces fixed costs per unit.

B. Focused Improvement—The Four-F Model

A Lightweight and Powerful Design Thinking Workshop

It used to be that we would say you can have it faster, better, or cheaper—pick any two. But going forward, that's not really an option. We need to do faster *and* better *and* cheaper to reach our organizational goals.

Innovation is one of those things that sometimes feels very elusive. It's not about some sort of a thunderclap or a lightning bolt in the middle of the night. It's not about sitting bolt upright and saying, "Eureka, I have found it! I know what we need to do." Sometimes that might happen, but that's not what we're after. What we are seeking is a purposeful approach that will put us in the right place, that will set us up with the right tools and enable us to methodically, clearly, and directly come up with innovations that will benefit us. We have either moved the ball forward, or we might be like Thomas Edison, who said, "I have not failed. I have merely found ten thousand ways to not create a light bulb." That's what we want to do. This can be a fun approach. I know that sounds funny, having fun at work, but let's dig into it.

First, let's look at what we mean by innovation. There are four "kinds" of innovation, and we use a simple model to outline the kind of innovation we want and the approach we want to take.

Transformational	Non-linear
Incremental	Linear

Table 2. Innovation types.

The type of innovation you need and how you need or want to address it is the driver for these flavors, and the process of understanding your approach will determine the model you use and how you use it. For our purposes here, we will look at this from an incremental, non-linear perspective. It will be incremental because we're going to look at how we can make an improvement in a current problem. If we wanted to completely redesign a product or change how we built something, we might choose a transformational innovation model or approach. In many cases, it is a choice of mindset versus a change in model.

We're also going to address this in our approach here as a non-linear innovation, as we're going to determine an improvement, and then we'll test or begin to use that improved version. If it works well, we may continue to use that for an indeterminate period of time and move on to the next issue we want to tackle. We might also choose to take that improvement a step further or try an alternate approach to solving the same issue. In other words, we'll iterate until we're satisfied. A linear approach might be to start at the top of the list and work our way through. Or we could take a linear approach that lines up the issues and addresses them collectively, perhaps like we "used to do" with a "waterfall" or serial approach. We might choose to do this, for example, because there is a high degree of dependency between them or because we need to do all the work at once due to resource constraints or implementation necessity.

Many of the innovation models or techniques used have specific objectives, tools, or approaches, such as personas. For our purposes, we're going to take one of the most lightweight models that will make it the easiest to use and most versatile. Our approach for this exercise doesn't use personas, which are extremely helpful for doing product development. However, over time, you might choose to identify persistent roles, whether on your team or interfacing groups, or representing other stakeholders, customers, or even competitors. Building a "library" like this over time can help you avoid missing an important or impactful perspective. However, an Agile development team or other iterative or sprint-based team using this system may have the same folks for every session, and they may be continuously immersed in the environment with the issue you want to address. For example, we use this approach today as part of our iteration retrospective to continuously drive improvement in our team processes.

The model is a classic flair-and-focus approach. In our flair, steps we'll drive for maximum volume of ideas and will not evaluate or edit any suggestions. More is better; quality or feasibility will not even be considered. In fact, we're going to encourage silly, flippant, and crazy ideas. Then we'll move into a focus mode, where we'll identify the one component, aspect, or portion of our topic and will "frame" that as the focal point. We'll flair again as we "brainstorm" about all of the things that could "move the needle" on the issue we're tackling. In fact, we will want to include things that move the needle the wrong way, just to make sure we're pushing the right button or pulling the right lever. Then, in the fourth and last step, we will once again focus on the approach that we're going to take. We like to call this "running the experiment." We think it will work. We have a hypothesis of the problem and solution, so we will test that to confirm the result.

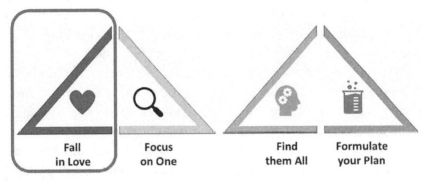

Image 20. Focused Improvement, Step 1: Fall in Love (with the Problem).

1. Fall in Love (with the Problem)

The first thing we want to do is make sure we fall in love with the problem. Now, it's really, really tempting to start jumping to conclusions and coming up with solutions before we've really vetted the problem. We can kind of think of this like an A3.[134] The first section that you fill out in an A3 is not the countermeasures; it is defining the problem. Let's do it now as an example exercise so we can walk through this. Think of a current problem that you have. Write it down (go ahead, we'll wait).

The first thing to do is to make sure you truly understand the problem. That's really what we're talking about here. We want you to totally immerse yourself into what that problem is. Now, the cool and interesting

---

[134] https://en.wikipedia.org/wiki/A3_problem_solving

part of this is that you are already doing that, because we're talking about addressing your problem. So, you're already immersed. It's not an academic issue. It's something that you're living, something that you're experiencing. However, we also know that other folks have different perspectives on this issue. We want to ensure we understand it from all those other perspectives, or as many as we can discover, define, and explore. We call this a "flair" process. We want to get as much information as we can, and there's no such thing as bad information. The more information we have about the problem and the different perspectives, the better. What are the folks upstream doing that affects the problem that you're addressing? What about the folks downstream? If you fix your problem, what does that do to, with, or for them? We want to make sure that we put on as many pairs of shoes as we can, right? Walk in the shoes of the other folks and see what it looks like from their perspective.

Who are the folks who have an input or are creating that problem? Whatever you're doing, who else is going to be involved in that? Is there anyone that's a recipient of or has a vested interest in the outcome? Think about it from their perspective. If you remember the movie *The Silence of the Lambs*,[135] Dr. Hannibal Lecter (played by Sir Anthony Hopkins) spent a lot of time with Agent Starling (played by Jodie Foster) trying to get to the root cause of the issue (they were investigating a murder). You may remember him chiding her, "No, no, no, those are symptoms. What is its nature?" What is the nature of the issue? What's the nature of the outcome? What's the nature of the problem that we're trying to solve? Have you got that in your mind now? Are you thinking about the other perspectives on your problem?

While we're doing that, let's think a little bit about Albert Einstein, arguably one of the smartest men who ever lived. He came up with ideas that we are only now beginning to be capable of understanding. In some cases, we are just now beginning to prove his theories. He said that if he had only one hour to work on a problem, he'd spend the first fifty-five minutes thinking about the problem, and then the answer would emerge—he'd only need five minutes to solve it. If it worked for

---

[135] https://en.wikipedia.org/wiki/The_Silence_of_the_Lambs_(film)

him, so maybe there's something in there that we can learn. Maybe we can be almost as smart as he was because we do this kind of thinking.

Another perspective might be to take the position of our "nemesis." Who is that person who is so critical of our ideas? They might actually be our best friend. They might be the best foil that we could have. What would they say about the problem? How would they try to shoot us down? What would they say about the solution we might have in mind? Would they say we are solving the right problem or that we are headed down the wrong path?

Okay. Now we've talked about the problem. We've talked about thinking about it from every possible perspective. However, are we sure we're actually solving the *right problem*? Let's think about this. Have you done any sort of root-cause analysis or evaluation to make sure you're tackling the right problem? If so, have you identified multiple problems and chosen one for a very specific reason, based what takes priority, where the hottest fire is, and what you're interested in, whatever that is. It doesn't really matter, as long as you recognize it for what it is, so we can move forward accordingly. However, we want to make sure that we're not just addressing symptoms. "What's the nature of it, Clarice?" Okay.

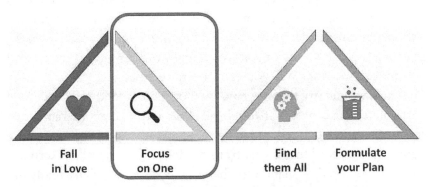

| Fall in Love | Focus on One | Find them All | Formulate your Plan |

Image 21. Focused Improvement, Step 2: Focus on One Thing.

2. Focus on One Thing

Do you have kids? Even if you don't, have you ever spent time with a four-year-old? If so, you probably know their favorite question: "Why?"

Why, why, why? At some point, most of us get to the point and say, "Because I'm your parent and I said so." But that's not really where we're going to go with this.

We know that from Six Sigma that we use the five whys, and it's just as applicable in this environment for all the same reasons. It's just as powerful in this space. So, once we identify the issue we want to address, we want to go from the flair (detailing as many different perspectives and as much information as we can) to the focus, homing in on the one thing. And we really want to get it down to one thing. What's the one thing that we really want to address in this? If any of you have been privileged to work with the consulting firm McKinsey, or if you've read *The McKinsey Mind*[136] or *The McKinsey Way*,[137] you already know how powerful a hypothesis can be and what that enables you to do. When you create a hypothesis, you have gone through the information; you've thought it through. You've identified what you think is the issue and what you think might be a way to address that. Then you can begin to evaluate the assumptions baked into that hypothesis and how you can test that hypothesis.

The more quickly you test and either prove or disprove (probably disprove) your original hypothesis, the better job you can do focusing on the one thing you want to address. And you might, in that hypothesis, even be able to identify (or at least begin to align yourself with) the levers we're going to pull (or that we can pull) with this hypothesis. What buttons can we push? What outcomes can we expect?

Once we identify that, we have our focal point (and the focal point is an interesting concept). If you think about it from a photography perspective, as you move closer to or farther away from your topic, the focal point changes. And that's what framing does for us as well. In terms of framing, we also then make sure that we're focused on what's really important to us. We want to focus our attention on just one thing, whatever is most interesting, most pertinent, or most powerful among the issues

---

[136] https://www.amazon.com/McKinsey-Mind-Understanding-Implementing-Problem-Solving/dp/0071374299
[137] https://www.amazon.com/McKinsey-Way-Ethan-M-Rasiel/dp/0070534489

we have uncovered as we "fell in love" with our problem. We want to understand the various perspectives of this, our current focal point.

We're going to talk a little bit about perspective. I'd like to share a video. It's actually been around for quite a while, but it's a very interesting video in terms of how our perspectives can change based on how we look at a problem:

Link: The Power of Perspective
https://youtu.be/0fKBhvDjuy0

If we reframe the problem and consider what we want to focus on—if we think about this from different perspectives like that—we don't have to go twenty-four light years away. We can just step back a few steps, step forward a few steps, and consider our perspectives.

The Power of One

So, we've asked you to identify just one thing, one idea, when we know there are thousands—hundreds of thousands—of things that we could do that would improve our processes, which would improve our environment, which would improve our ability to deliver, our tools, whatever it is that we want to do. But why just one? Read about the fifty-two–week penny challenge to see an example of "just one."

Exercise: The Fifty-Two–Week Penny Challenge
https://www.savingadvice.com/articles/2014/
01/01/1019727_365-day-money-challenge.html

It's a very simple and powerful demonstration of what "just one" can do for us, one thing for us to focus on at a time. The idea is that beginning on any given day, you start off with putting a penny into a jar, or piggy bank, or whatever. The next day, you match what you put in the day before, and you add one more penny. We can think of this as the ideas that we've already accumulated. We don't throw away the idea that we had yesterday or last week. We continue to use it. We continue to benefit from that, and we add just one more idea to that. On the first day, we put in one penny, and on the very last day, we put in 365 pennies. Do you see the math? It is very straightforward.

Each day we have one idea to add to yesterday's idea. It's not exactly the same as compounding, but conceptualizing it that way is directionally correct, because just as we compounded money in that example, we really are compounding our ideas. The total comes to $667.95. I don't know about you, but I was rather surprised when I saw that number the first time. This is a clue as to why we really want to focus on one idea. Let's not turn it into an entire thesis. We don't need to take this beyond a short conversation. We want to come up with one idea, and especially if we're empowered with the concept "It doesn't even have to be right." Remember, it is important that we allow and encourage people to fail fast, fail forward, and learn. We want to test it because we may prove one of the ten thousand ways not to create a light bulb.

Next, we move on to the fun part of the process: "Find Them All."

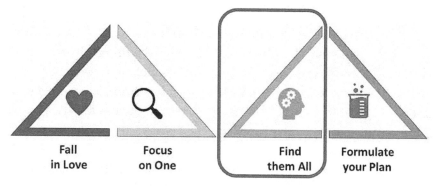

| Fall in Love | Focus on One | Find them All | Formulate your Plan |

Image 22. Focused Improvement, Step 3: Find Them All.

3. Find Them All

Do you remember playing hide and seek and going on scavenger hunts? They were so much fun, giving us the opportunity to explore and find new things. An interesting idea about what makes us laugh when we hear a funny joke or saying, is that it is the result of the "feel good" hormones being released when we make a new connection between previously unassociated concepts. Maybe it's why it can be such a thrill to meet someone new and exciting or visit someplace we've never been before.

Again, we want to go into a flair mode. We want as many ideas as we possibly can get about what we could do to address that particular lever, to prove or disprove our hypothesis. In many respects, it's a lot like the brainstorming we talked about in the past, right? It's about quantity; it's about getting as many ideas as we can. And we don't want to edit them as we go. We don't want to evaluate them. We certainly don't want to shut anybody down because we think that their idea is silly or stupid or whatever. There are some tools that can use to help us to get there. "Yes, and …" is one of them. Are you familiar with that one? It is a standard practice in the world of improvisation (comedy or theater), but it goes beyond that, and we'll look at that much more explicitly in just a moment.

I'll share with you a story where I found this technique to be particularly fun. A couple of years ago, I was fortunate enough to spend some time with Nordstrom. There, we used this approach to look at different kinds of services that they could introduce to improve their customer retention. It's certainly no secret that Nordstrom, and most other brick-and-mortar stores, are having an increasingly difficult time in the marketplace, especially up against Amazon and organizations like that. So, looking at how they can improve their service and engage customers is incredibly important to them. That's what we were focused on. What happened was very normal: groups of friends got together and had fun with what they were doing. One particular group of friends had just come back from a weekend in Mexico. They were all about "Mike, the hot bartender" from their favorite place in Cancun. Their choice of topic was to look at the cosmetics section of the stores.

They said, "We really hate the way we do cosmetics. It's at the front of the store, where we're on display, like we're at the zoo. It's got all this harsh fluorescent lighting, and we really can't sit there and have fun with it. So, what if we put it in the back of the store?"

Then one of them popped up with "The store, yeah, yeah, yeah. Let's put a bar in. Let's just get Mike, the hot bartender to come out and we'll have fun. We'll have a little party back there and do our makeup and try different things." They laughed about it, and then they said, "Yeah, that's actually sounds like a good idea." It worked quite well for them for (at least for a while, as far as I know).

The key to that was using "Yes, and …" Yes, let's have a bar in the back with Mike, the hot bartender, and then we can actually have more fun with the cosmetics, try more things and not feel as if we're on display. Get folks more engaged. They'll want to come in and do this and not just because they have to, because they are out of this or need that. And that's where the fun can really come in to drive synergy.

As we said, we really want to drive the quantity of ideas. More is better. We really do not want to think about quality because with the "Yes, and…" approach, we can deconstruct that. We can take that silly, flippant, crazy idea, combine it with something that's not so silly, flippant, or crazy, and come up with some really interesting things. We really want you to go crazy with it. "Yes, and …" is a very powerful tool in this. "Yes, and …" says, "Yeah, I heard you. I'm good with that. I may not understand it. It may not seem to make sense, but with the 'and,' I can add something to that." So, we're going to accept their ideas, and so, "Yes, and …" is an incredibly powerful tool for us in so many different ways. We want to encourage folks, even push them, to come up with some of the silly, crazy, flippant ideas that we can then combine with other things.

Video links for "Yes, and …":

- Bob Kulhan: Improv 101 (The "Yes, and … " Principle): https://youtu.be/DphjhudlZis
- Two words that can change the world, YES AND: Karen Tilstra at TEDxOrlando: https://youtu.be/l1SK_qNLx5U

Once we start that ball rolling, once we start throwing out flippant ideas, like getting the bartender from Cancun to come up and help us sell cosmetics, we also can inspire others with those ideas. We can make them feel free and safe to come up with silly, flippant, crazy ideas, and we can then combine those ideas with something a little more down to earth. Then we really come up with a different way of looking at the problem, a really creative way of solving that problem. We are also going to become at least a little bit vulnerable. If we're going to throw out a silly idea like that, we have to be prepared for and understand that somebody might laugh at that idea of ours. And that's okay.

But why is that okay? Because when we become vulnerable like that, we put ourselves "out there." We're expecting (and hopefully we're going to experience) the fact that our team doesn't take advantage of that vulnerability. In fact, we encourage them to be vulnerable as well. When we share vulnerability, we grow the bonds between us. We can deepen the ties with our team as we move forward. We can build the kinds of relationships that say, "Hey, I can let this all hang out, and we're all going to be okay with that," and you can too. In a very short period, we're going to be able to communicate better. We're going to be able to work together more smoothly. We're going to be able to understand that we may not agree. In fact, we might be vigorously opposed, and we might fight about it tooth and nail, but we're going to focus on the topic and not the people, because we've developed that relationship. We can have a high-trust environment because we've been vulnerable, and we've been protected. We've seen people be vulnerable, and we've accepted that, and we've embraced them, and in that way, we can really improve the strength of our teams.

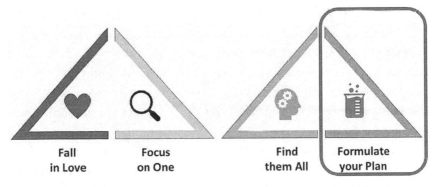

Image 23. Focused Improvement, Step 4: Formulate Your Plan.

4. Formulate Your Plan

Next, we want to try a prototype. We want to do something very small that will take that idea that we've come up with and to put it into action, test it out and try it. This should be really simple. You can think of this as sort of the "crepe paper, construction paper, and popsicle sticks" proto-type approach. It doesn't have to be fancy; it doesn't have to be electronic. It should be just something as simple and as "quick and dirty" as we can possibly make it to get at the hypothesis, prove that out, and test the idea that we've settled on. Let's be clear here too: this is *your* plan. You need to come up with your plan. You need to put the pieces in place to test your plan. You need to evaluate the results of your plan. Own it. There is no "they"!

We can even take it a step further. Have you ever heard of the "How might we?" approach? "How might we?" is a powerful verbal construct, and it is incredible when used synergistically with "Yes, and..." The following videos explore this concept.

Video links for "How might we?":

- Sara Thurber and FourSightOnline[138]: https://youtu.be/6BfIK3suMBo
- Level Up with EP - How Might We?: https://youtu.be/mRpUV-uIkF8

You might also think about trying it with another team. Maybe the line that's adjacent to yours or a team upstairs or across the aisle. You try their idea, and they try your idea. Then you get somebody else's perspective on that prototype or that testing process, and that's how we can forward it for experimentation. Then we "run the experiment." You did your prototype. Did you get the result that you expected, somewhere near it, maybe the inverse? Okay. That's good. From time to time, you'll get it wrong, and that's a good thing. We want to "embrace the fail." We want people to feel safe trying something different. If you fail, moving the needle you had in mind but moving at the wrong way, then we can say, "Yes, we have found the lever. But we pushed it instead of pulling it." If we get it right, especially if we get it sort of right or mostly right, then we might not get as much of an advantage as if we got it wrong, because we probably won't go back and reevaluate that, in which case we might miss the opportunity for a real breakthrough.

---

[138] https://foursightonline.com/

So, now we've got two very powerful tools in our quiver or our tool-box. If we take the "Yes, and …"—those inspirational, crazy ideas—and marry them with something much more down to- earth, that actually addresses our situation directly in the context of a business issue, then coupled that with "How might we?" solutions, we've created a powerful tool for us to explore. If we then compare this to the hypothesis we generated at the very beginning, all of a sudden, we are seriously driving innovation.

Learn more about Focused Improvement – the 4F model, and get more help at www.FocusedImprovement.us.

C. Follow-Up and Additional Material

Keys to Driving Enterprise DevOps Improvements

Okay, you're here either because you've implemented DevOps and you're looking for what's next or you're planning ahead (good for you!).

As enterprises move to adopt DevOps practices, they will want to measure where teams are on their journey. This sometimes leads to the development of maturity models used to assess teams' levels and progress. While I am not going to pass judgment on what might be useful for certain organizations, I believe that the real key is to drive continuous improvement through data like lead time, frequency of deployments, and MTTR (i.e., the key metrics from the "State of DevOps" reports[139]).

Any static maturity model will become outdated. What's more important is that teams are taught concepts that will help them continuously evaluate obstacles to delivering more quickly so that they identify areas for improvement. The key to this is the lean concept of value-stream analysis. If you walk up to a team and ask them why they can't go faster, they will typically say they are waiting for something. They could be waiting for more work to flow into their backlog. They could be waiting for the infrastructure needed for development or testing. Or they could be waiting for another team to develop a service they need to consume.

Many teams don't spend time in retrospectives talking about how to overcome these types of blockers (or wait states) and developing countermeasures as continuous-improvement initiatives. One reason for this is the lack of objective data that one can analyze to gain insights on this. This is where the lead-time metric comes into play. Historically, lead time has been defined as (last) code commit to deploy into production. While this is important, it tells only part of the story, because accelerated delivery and feedback really start with getting a customer concept and measuring how long this takes until it is delivered into production, so feedback can be provided.

One challenge to providing this kind of end-to-end metric, which spans the entire delivery value stream, is the lack of an integrated delivery pipeline from which data can be automatically collected. A customer

---

[139] https://puppet.com/resources/whitepaper/state-of-devops-report

concept starts in the portfolio space, which might result in data being entered in some type of PPM (project and portfolio management) system. Once approved, this will result in features being created that should eventually flow into a product backlog. Stories are then created that can be pulled by the Agile team supporting that product into an iteration. This information is typically in some Agile management system (e.g., Jira or IBM Rational Team Concert). Then the team develops and builds the stories, tests them, and deploys them into production via a deployment tool like UrbanCode. So, this flow of work goes through various tooling and is generally not visible or easily traceable across the value stream.

Value-stream analysis must differentiate the time spent adding value to product being created (referred to a "process time") from the time spent in wait states. An example of process time in the IT delivery value stream is time spent writing the stories, coding, and testing. Once teams gain more insight into what is slowing them down, they can identify countermeasures they can apply. Examples of wait times are the time a story spends in the backlog and the time a finished build must wait until it can be deployed into production.

Categories of wait states include

- Waiting for a dependent area to provide functionality necessary to complete a feature
- Service-level agreements (SLAs) associated with a service provided by a centralized organization (e.g., performance testing or security testing)
- SLAs associated with infrastructure needed for an environment
- Contention for a shared test environment

Countermeasures associated with these types of wait states are

- Architecture decoupling
- Dark launching/feature-toggling
- Expanding cross-functional teams to enable them to do self-service performance and security testing (at least some portion of it)
- Automated provisioning capability for environment to avoid wait states and contention

The "State of DevOps Report 2017"[140] contains information about the importance of architecture and how decoupling dependencies (using APIs and microservices) can mitigate certain types of wait states. "DevOps Case Studies"[141] provides more information on applying practices such as dark launching.

But again, at the heart of this is getting teams to think more about what their value stream actually looks like, how long it takes to deliver business value that can generate feedback, and what is preventing them from going faster. This is not a technology play. This is not something that somebody can sell or educate you on. This is something that must be taken on by the team itself.

The team can start by educating themselves on some of these concepts using a book club. A great place to start is to study *The Phoenix Project*.[142] This novel approach combines aspects of both DevOps and lean to drive home some key points in the journey to discover types of work, manage WIP (work in progress), and ultimately improve visibility of and control over the work being done for the business. Once a team has an understanding of their value stream and blockers, they can then study *The DevOps Handbook*,[143] which provides practical guidance for improving their delivery capability and speed.

Deming—Worth a Deeper Look

A great deal of this book builds on the work of Deming, without whom we would probably not be talking about many of the topics within. The breadth and depth of his work is impressive, and we would do well to master half his expertise. I suggest you consider Deming as your sensei through this journey.

> William Edwards Deming (October 14, 1900— December 20, 1993) was an American engineer, statistician, professor, author, lecturer, and management

---

[140] https://puppet.com/resources/whitepaper/state-of-devops-report
[141] https://itrevolution.com/book/devops-case-studies/
[142] https://itrevolution.com/book/the-phoenix-project/
[143] https://itrevolution.com/book/the-devops-handbook/

consultant. Educated initially as an electrical engineer and later specializing in mathematical physics, he helped develop the sampling techniques still used by the U.S. Department of the Census and the Bureau of Labor Statistics. In his book, "The New Economics for Industry, Government, and Education," Deming championed the work of Walter Shewhart, including statistical process control, operational definitions, and what Deming called the "Shewhart Cycle" which had evolved into Plan-Do-Study-Act (PDSA). This was in response to the growing popularity of PDCA, which Deming viewed as tampering with the meaning of Shewhart's original work. Deming is best known for his work in Japan after WWII, particularly his work with the leaders of Japanese industry. That work began in August 1950 at the Hakone Convention Center in Tokyo, when Deming delivered a speech on what he called "Statistical Product Quality Administration." Many in Japan credit Deming as one of the inspirations for what has become known as the Japanese post-war economic miracle of 1950 to 1960, when Japan rose from the ashes of war on the road to becoming the second-largest economy in the world through processes partially influenced by the ideas Deming taught.[144]

After the Second World War, Deming was sent to Japan as a consultant, where these ideas took root. Before long, Japan was producing products (e.g., cars) whose quality exceeded those made in other countries. It wasn't until the 1980s, when faced with market pressures, that these ideas caught on in United States.

Deming taught that "quality is everyone's responsibility," which was a new concept, since the accepted thinking was that quality was something that was accomplished through testing rather than built into the

---

[144] "W. Edwards Deming," *Wikipedia*, last updated July 5, 2018, https://en.wikipedia.org/wiki/W._Edwards_Deming.

product. Deming's teachings also dealt with management as well as quality. Contrary to generally accepted ideas, his goal was not to improve the present style of management by adding a new component *but to transform management practices from top to bottom.*

At the core of this was his concept of developing a system of profound knowledge that was necessary to achieve the transformation.

Deming suggested that US companies generally were afflicted with seven deadly diseases that gave their competitors an advantage until they were understood and eliminated:

1. *Lack in constancy of purpose* to plan and deliver products and services that will help a company survive in the long term
2. *Emphasis on short-term profits* caused by short-term thinking (which is just the opposite of constancy of purpose), fear of takeovers, worry about quarterly dividends, and other types of reactive management
3. *Performance appraisals that promote fear* and stimulate unnecessary competition among employees
4. *Mobility of management (i.e., job hopping),* which promotes short-term thinking
5. *Management by use of visible figures* without concern about other data, such as the effect of happy and unhappy customers on sales, and the increase in overall quality and productivity that comes from quality improvement upstream
6. *Excessive medical costs*
7. *Excessive costs of liability* further increased by lawyers working on contingency fees

To counter these deadly diseases, Deming created fourteen points that he believed a company's leaders should adhere to in order to have successful quality management. Some methods we use today as part of Agile, Lean, and DevOps to accomplish these are listed with the items below:

1. **Create constancy of purpose** toward improvement of product and service → *Development of standard work (Lean)*

2. **We must prevent mistakes** → *Lean/Agile principles of design quality into the product*
3. **Cease dependence on mass inspection. Instead, design and build in quality** → *Test-driven development, automated test-driven development*
4. **Minimize total cost** → *Lower total cost of ownership through fewer defects and lower run costs*
5. **Continuously improve** the system of production and service → *Continuous Improvement/A3 practices*
6. **Institute training** → *Adult-learning model (Gene Kim's third way)*
7. **Institute leadership** (modern methods of supervision). The best supervisors are leaders and coaches, not dictators → *Servant leadership*
8. **Create a fear-free environment where everyone can contribute and work effectively** → *Focus on associate engagement and net promoter scores ("State of DevOps Report")*
9. **Eliminate barriers through better communication, cross-functional teams, and changing attitudes and cultures** → *Cross-functional teams with product owners*
10. **Understand that most problems are system-related and require managerial involvement to rectify or change** → *Continuous improvement /A3 practices*
11. **Learn the capabilities of processes and how to improve them** → *Standard work*
12. **Remove barriers that hinder workers** → *Lean practices*
13. **Institute a vigorous program of education and self-improvement** → *Continuous Learning*
14. **Create a structure in top management that will promote the previous thirteen points**

Deming drew upon the PDCA model developed by his colleague at Bell Laboratories, Dr. Walter A. Shewhart. This is the model upon which the Six Sigma DMAIC (define, measure, analyze, improve, and control) improvement cycle is built.

Some common pitfalls described by Deming include

1. Assuming a process is under control without having any measures to validate this
2. Setting objectives without a good (factual/data based) understanding of what the process is capable of (or if it is even under tight control)
3. Analyzing and taking corrective actions of situations that fall within normal control limits ("knee-jerk" reactions to common cause situations)
4. Using data as a primary measure of people's performance rather than process performance (lead time, frequency of deployment)
5. Setting an expectation to achieve better results without targeting what process improvements are needed to achieve those results
6. Implementing changes based on intuition or subjective information
7. Not having data to identify root causes (e.g., many defects but no way to determine what is responsible for this, such as poor code quality)
8. Implementing changes without the ability to measure impacts
9. Failing to utilize practitioner input as a primary source to drive continuous improvement (CI)

This last item is an area where companies often err because they don't utilize associate input to drive improvement activities. As discussed in the chapters on "Culture," it is the team itself that knows best how to improve, while leaders need to apply systems thinking to optimize the entire system.

So, while Deming certainly paved the way for the practices that are now part of Agile and DevOps, perhaps Dickens back in 1859 also had a glimpse into the future. Let's make ourselves the selfless heroes that lead these transformations and hope that we have the courage of Carton[145] without having to suffer the same fate.

---

[145] https://en.wikipedia.org/wiki/Sydney_Carton

EPILOGUE

As we work through the content herein, we as leaders must rely on our experience and ability to apply these concepts appropriately for our organization. The days of planning our transitions and transformations to the nth degree are long behind us, and for good reason. We no longer have the opportunity to define our future; we can merely help to guide it. Make no mistake, this doesn't mean that we just "go with the flow." Instead, we share our vision and help our teams find that vision with the influences of the market, new thinking, technology, and the strength of our people. Meanwhile, we need to gain a deeper understanding to help drive sustainability and continue our role as leaders so that we can be the *ri* our organizations need.

INDEX

A

Agile x, 2, 13, 14, 15, 16, 17, 35, 45, 67, 94
Agile Manifesto 14, 15
Albert Einstein 132
Amazon 1, 137
Amazon Web Services 77
American Medical Association 55
API(s) 69, 80, 83, 84, 85, 86, 87, 89, 144
application performance monitoring 45
apprentice 35
AppScan 99
architecture 76, 77, 86, 104, 143
Atlassian 80
audit(s) 27, 28, 30
authentic 32, 37, 89, 95
automation 5, 21, 27, 29, 34, 44, 65, 69, 92, 113
Automation Anywhere 100
availability 1, 27, 28, 105, 106, 107, 108
AWS 7

B

backlog 9, 11, 12, 13, 24, 25, 62, 67, 80, 85, 142, 143
baseline 4, 48
batch sizes 67, 68
behavior modification 37

Bell Labs 22, 81, 83, 86, 94, 105, 111, 112
big bang 25
blockers 9, 13, 69, 142, 144
Blue Prism 100
Borg Warner 35
bottleneck 18, 75
business portfolio 25
business value 23, 79

C

capacity 12, 13, 22, 38, 70, 75, 89, 112
Capital One 1, 7, 99
Captain Crunch 114, 115
Carole Robin 44
certification 29, 30
chaos monkey 108, 112
Charles Dickens 93
Chip and Dan Heath 40
CI 96, 148
Cindy Payne 95
clarity 21
Clarity 101
CMMI 63
Cobol 77
code repository 28
collaboration 11, 21, 39, 70, 71
commander's Intent 90
commitment 71
competitive advantage 9, 15, 49, 50, 51, 56

CPSIA information can be obtained
at www.ICGtesting.com
Printed in the USA
LVHW082110110219
607156LV00029B/959/P